Language and Law

Annabelle Mooney

Reader in the Department of Media, Culture and Language,
University of Roehampton, UK

palgrave
macmillan

First published 2014 by
PALGRAVE MACMILLAN

Palgrave Macmillan in the UK is an imprint of Macmillan Publishers Limited,
registered in England, company number 785998, of Houndmills, Basingstoke,
Hampshire RG21 6XS.

Palgrave Macmillan in the US is a division of St Martin's Press LLC,
175 Fifth Avenue, New York, NY 10010.

Palgrave Macmillan is the global academic imprint of the above companies
and has companies and representatives throughout the world.

Palgrave® and Macmillan® are registered trademarks in the United States,
the United Kingdom, Europe and other countries

ISBN: 978–1–137–01794–9

This book is printed on paper suitable for recycling and made from fully
managed and sustained forest sources. Logging, pulping and manufacturing
processes are expected to conform to the environmental regulations of the
country of origin.

A catalogue record for this book is available from the British Library.

A catalog record for this book is available from the Library of Congress.

Typeset by Cambrian Typesetters, Camberley, Surrey

Printed in China

Contents

Contents   vii

Tables, Figures and Images

Acknowledgements

While I am not a forensic linguist, I have long been interested in how law uses language. I have been very fortunate to meet a number of people who have both inspired me and indulged my many questions. While I was taking my PhD, I worked for Professor Sheila McLean; as well as being a generous and forgiving boss, seeing her work in the field of law and ethics in medicine taught me how important law is for real people. Indeed, everyone at the Institute for Law and Ethics in Medicine at the University of Glasgow contributed to my decision to work on law; thank you. Andrea Jarman and Patricia Glass, who have always been patient with my naive questions about law, as have the scholars who participate in the International Roundtables for the Semiotics of Law. I have been very fortunate in being allowed to teach Forensic Linguistics at the University of Roehampton, where I inherited a beautiful course from Dr Frances Rock. Learning how to teach this class has given me a great deal of pleasure, and my students have provided considered points of view about much of the material in this book. I would like to thank Dr Betsy Evans for help with the chapter on forensic phonetics (all errors are naturally mine) as well as for her endless and expert advice and support. Thank you to Amanda Iveson for the example of a very minimal narrative in Chapter 9. Conversations with Professor Gerlinde Mautner about law are always energising and exciting, I would also like to thank her, along with Dr Fiona English and Dr Tim Grant for making their research available to me in advance of publication. Thank you also to Paul Stevens and Aléta Bezuidenhout at Palgrave Macmillan who have been supportive, patient and terribly helpful. Finally, I wouldn't be able to do much of anything at all without the support of my partner, Dr Christopher Marlow.

Sources

Example 1.1 and Example 1.2 reproduced with permission from Transport for London (TfL) © Transport for London.

Image 1.1 reproduced with permission from Transport for London (TfL) © Transport for London.

Example 1.3 is reproduced under terms of the Open Government Licence v1.0.

Figure 1.1 and Figure 1.2 are from Sebeok, Thomas A., *Style in Language*, modified versions of figures from pages 353 and 357, © 1960 Massachusetts Institute of Technology, by permission of The MIT Press.

The extract on p. 20 is reproduced with kind permission from Rahul Roushan, *Faking News*

Example 6.1 is reproduced with the kind permission of Equinox Publishing Limited.

Table 3.1 is reproduced with the kind permission of Equinox Publishing Limited.

Examples 4.4 and 4.5 are reproduced with the kind permission of Equinox Publishing Limited.

Example 6.2 is reproduced with kind permission of The Rowman & Littlefield Publishing Group.

Example 6.3, example 6.4 and example 6.5 are from Hale, Sandra. 'How faithfully do court interpreters render the style of non-English speaking witnesses' testimonies? A data-based study of Spanish-English bilingual proceedings.' *Discourse Studies* 4 (1) (2002): 25–47 © 2002 Sage Publications, by permission of SAGE.

The example in Activity 6.4 is reproduced with the kind permission of Cambridge University Press.

Examples 6.6 and 6.7 are from English, Fiona. 'Non-native speakers in detention: Assessing non-native speaking detainees' English Language proficiency.' *Handbook of Forensic Linguistics*. Eds. Malcolm Coulthard and Alison Johnson. Oxford: Routledge, 2010. pp. 432–39. Reproduced with kind permission of Routledge.

Table 10.1 is reproduced with the permission of Springer Science + Business Media.

Image 10.1 is reproduced under terms of the Open Government Licence v1.0.

Image 10.2 is reproduced with the kind permission of Elizabeth Miller and under terms of the Open Government Licence v1.0.

Image 10.3 is reproduced under terms of the Open Government Licence v1.0.

Image 10.4 is reproduced under terms of the Open Government Licence v1.0.

Preface

Welcome to the first volume in Language &..., a series of accessible and thought-provoking textbooks by leading scholars. Each volume in the series aims to provide students with a stimulating and engaging introduction to the best new thinking about language, to refine, redefine and critique ideas about language and to encourage questioning and active learning.

The texts are designed to provide a quick but thorough introduction to sites, spaces, concepts, processes and methodologies in understanding the inter-related, interdependent role of language in everyday life – but to do so using an innovative and problem-based approach that will engage readers' interests and develop critical thinking and other transferable skills.

The volumes in the series examine language from a variety of perspectives. The first volumes in the series focus on *sites and spaces*, exploring the ways that language use takes place in, and is shaped by, specific sites, professional fields and relationships. The current volume focuses on Language & Law, and forthcoming volumes will focus on topics such as Language & Business, Language & Media, and Language & Journalism. As the series develops, we will continue to expand the coverage of sites and spaces, but will also move on to volumes dealing with *concepts* integral to the understanding of language, how it works and how it can be investigated; *processes* that shape and are shaped by language use; and *methodologies* – innovative ways of investigating language.

The series is primarily designed to appeal to students of languages, linguistics and communications, and participants in sociolinguistics modules in general or specialist degrees. Secondarily, it will appeal to those in domain- or site-specific subjects (e.g. journalism), who need an understanding of the role language plays in their professional field or specific focus of interest. For this reason, the Language & ... textbooks do not assume any prior knowledge of linguistics on the part of the reader.

In this first volume, Annabelle Mooney highlights the centrality of language to the legal system and also shows how legal process underpins

so many of our discursive routines in everyday life. Mooney demonstrates how legal texts are not just found in courtrooms and parlia-
mentary archives but are all around us.

We are delighted that such a fascinating and significant site is the
focus of the first volume in the series.

HELEN KELLY-HOLMES AND SARI PIETIKÄINEN

Introduction

This is a book about language and law. Neither is easy to define, but I begin by offering some working definitions of both as well as providing some context for the study of both together. I also give some information about the structure of the book and explain some of the features that have been included.

While the law can be defined in a number of ways, fundamentally it is a system of rules with authority and force behind them. It is ultimately 'a *formal* mechanism of social control' (Slapper and Kelly, 2004, p. 2). Law most obviously connects with language in that it takes form and exerts control through language; legislation, judicial decisions and regulations all depend on language for their realisation and communication. In short, 'Law is a profession of words' (Mellinkoff, 1987, p. vii). It is, therefore, not surprising that linguists should be interested in law and all its linguistic manifestations. Moreover, the tools and approaches that linguists have developed in other contexts are well suited to the analysis of legal language, as well as to the analysis of language used in legal contexts. But because the law relies so much on language, legal professionals have their own views about how language works and this varies depending on the speaker or writer and the communicative context. For example, the way lawyers use language in court differs from the way police officers use language when speaking to the public. Thus, it is important to note that the law is neither homogenous nor singular. While it is possible to talk about 'the law' in a general and abstract way, what 'the law' means and how it is realised linguistically depends on context; on what is being done, to whom and where. Legal language has a number of faces.

Like law, language can also be described in terms of rules. Linguists pay attention to the way in which language systems are structured and used. That is not to say that the rules of language are the same as the rules of law. The rules of language describe what people do with language; they are found by analysing how people use language. The rules of law, on the other hand, set out how people should behave. Linguistic rules are ultimately descriptive while legal rules are prescriptive.

The title of this book, *Language and Law*, is intended to include not only instances of language which sets out the law (e.g. legislation) but also the use of language in legal contexts. This includes the language used by police when interviewing a suspect, the language used in courtrooms by lawyers and judges, as well as instances of language use which may be illegal (threats) or required (warnings). Attention is also paid to the use of different languages and how these are interpreted and translated, especially in the courtroom. Thus, a more appropriate way to approach the content here is to think of both law and language in both their plural and adjectival forms.

The area of language and the law is a broad one. It comes under the heading of Applied Linguistics, in that linguistic tools are used to analyse language that occurs in a legal context or to examine language that has legal consequences. Research is also conducted within the field of Language for Specific Purposes (LSP). Thus it is a diverse area and, perhaps as a result of this, it is difficult to identify or name a single object of study (Kurzon, 1997). This book seeks to provide a sense of the breadth of all this work as well as provide an insight into the kinds of details that linguists are interested in when dealing with language and the law.

The book is arranged with two things in mind. First, each chapter deals primarily with either a linguistic concept or an analytic method. Second, the chapters generally cover a part of the legal process. With the exception of the first and final chapters, the legal process is ordered in the way it would be experienced. Thus, Chapter 2 deals with written legal language, and Chapter 3 looks at speech acts that may also be crimes. The chapters that follow examine interactions with the police, before considering language in the courtroom, the issues that arise when the court becomes a multilingual environment, the role of linguists as experts in cases and the final stages of a trial.

I begin by showing that legal language is everywhere. Even the most mundane activities can involve legal language. This does not mean it will be easy to find or understand. That is, while some encounters obviously involve legal language, in other places it is necessary to go looking for it. The first chapter shows that two common preconceptions about legal language – that it is technical and only found in particular contexts – are unfounded. Indeed, an important skill for anyone looking closely at language is to be ready to be surprised, to be able to come to a piece of language without any preconceptions. Because of the preconceptions people tend to have, it seems to me that this is a particularly valuable approach when it comes to legal language. In this first chapter, I explain Jakobson's model of language to show that legal language, like 'ordinary' language, has a number of functions. Moreover, understanding the basic syntagmatic and paradigmatic axes of language that Jakobson draws attention to can be useful in analysing legal language. Thus, attention is paid to these axes of combination and some terminology for describing syntactic structure is provided.

Chapter 2 deals with written legal language, particularly that found in legislation and contracts. This kind of legal language is characterised by features such as nominalisation and complex syntactic structure. It also has its own vocabulary. This can be particularly challenging as it sometimes intersects with 'normal' language. While efforts are made to simplify legal language, especially for lay audiences, legal language can nevertheless be understood as a parallel linguistic world.

The third chapter introduces speech act theory by examining threats and warnings. These speech acts have received attention from researchers in language and law because of the illegality of some threats and the legal requirement for comprehensible warnings (especially in the case of consumer goods). Paying attention to speech acts which are familiar helps to understand how they work and shows why they are important in a legal context. Indeed, speech acts are central to the law's authority; laws are passed and people found guilty through the use of speech acts.

Grice's co-operative principle and its associated maxims are covered in Chapter 4. Grice's co-operative principle explains how communication occurs and also helps in articulating the different rules that may apply when dealing with authority figures like the police. This chapter looks at public interaction with police officers as well as what is involved in more formal suspect interviews with the police. This includes consideration of what it means to be silent, what rights a detainee has and whether she is likely to understand these rights.

Chapter 5 continues to examine interactions with the police by examining how witness statements are constructed. This chapter also introduces some concepts from conversation analysis by considering material from the courtroom, specifically, the way lawyers ask questions during examination-in-chief/direct examination and cross-examination. Extended examples are discussed to show not only the role of individual questions, but also the importance of the 'line' of questioning. Lawyers exploit question type and question order when making arguments in the courtroom.

Chapter 6 considers another important issue that arises in the courtroom context: the use of other languages. Attention is given to the difficulties of interpreting in the courtroom as well as to the rules that different language varieties rely on. Considering the challenges that interpreters face is important both for individuals involved in legal proceedings as well as for access to justice more generally. Moreover, there is a great deal that could be done to improve the working conditions of these professionals. The role of linguists in identifying a person's origin on the basis of her language is also covered, as this is sometimes an important part of granting asylum. It also shows the difficulty of locating languages in geographic terms.

Linguists are sometimes called to be expert witnesses or to help with police investigations; Chapters 7 and 8 explore the kinds of tasks that they are asked to undertake. Chapter 7 deals with spoken texts, and details the techniques that forensic phoneticians use, while Chapter 8 looks at written texts. The problems that confront expert linguists when explaining their work in written reports and in court are also examined.

Chapter 9 deals with narrative. Narratives are important in the examination of witnesses and judicial instructions to the jury. This chapter shows that narratives do more than simply report on events; they can also make arguments and play a part in the presentation of evidence. The narratives told about a trial may also have an effect on how the public understand the legal and social relevance of particular cases and the law more generally.

Finally, Chapter 10 deals with physical signs. This is a relatively new area for scholars in language and the law, but attention to signs demonstrates that they often depend on the law for their existence and authority. I deal with both written and spoken signs in order to show how both construct space and the audience they address.

In all chapters, activities are included that are designed to ask questions about a particular issue or to invite close attention to the detail an example. 'Real' legal material has been used where possible. The legal examples in this book are largely from Britain and related common law jurisdictions (e.g., USA, Australia, Canada and New Zealand) as this is the system which typifies English-speaking countries and also the law with which I am most familiar. Nevertheless, do bear in mind that legal language – as well as language with legal under-pinnings and effects – is all around us. I hope the examples included help you to find other cases of legal language and to explore the rich scholarly work in this field. The references in the chapters can be used for further reading. Finally, I use the generic 'she' in part to counter a common legal insistence on the generic 'he'. However, when referring to specific examples, I use pronouns consistent with the speaker's sex.

Both language and the law are omnipresent. Similarly, they do not tend to attract attention until something goes wrong. People ordinar-ily do not question their ability to communicate with other people and they tend not to pay continuous attention to the legal regimes which structure their world. It is worth doing, however, as paying attention to language in a legal context may have important consequences for justice and society and for the rights and responsibilities of citizens. This book can only scratch the surface of the issues, questions and research in the area of language and the law. But I hope it shows that looking at both the obvious and hidden legal language in the world and considering its legal effects is fascinating, frustrating and enter-taining. While searching for material for this book I discovered a judge who sentenced a husband to take his wife on a date (McShane, 2012), the importance of the meaning of 'the' (Hill, Lloyd and Goldman, 2012) and the sophisticated linguistic skills of barristers (Crowley, 2007). While some of the things I encountered were certainly amusing, they were also instructive. The power of judges, the importance of the defi-nite article and the application of abstract rules to specific cases can all be considered in terms of linguistic theory. I hope this book leads to your own discoveries in language and the law.

1

Finding the language

Legal language is sometimes very obvious and easy to find. When being arrested by the police or signing a contract, the language is clearly related to the law. But legal language may also be entirely invisible. Boarding a bus, for example, may not involve any language at all. However, once a person is allowed to get on the bus, a contract has been formed. These contracts contain a number of terms and conditions, setting out the rights and responsibilities of both the passenger and the bus company. Unless something goes wrong, this legal language remains hidden. Nevertheless, if one starts looking it is possible to find it. Once one is aware that rules exist it is possible to investigate them in more detail.

A travel pass commonly used in London is the Oyster card. On the front it states: 'Issued subject to conditions – see over'. Turning the card over, one finds:

Example 1.1

The issue and use of this Oyster card [the name of the travel pass] is subject to TfL's [Transport for London's] Conditions of Carriage, copies of which are available at any of our ticket outlets, or on our Customer Services web site at www.oystercard.com or the Oyster card helpline [telephone number]. Where this Oyster card is also valid for use on another operator's services, the Conditions of Carriage of that operator will apply in relation to travel on its service. Copies may be obtained from those operators (Transport for London).

If a passenger reads the card, and finds out that terms and conditions exist, some effort will still be required to ascertain exactly what these terms and conditions are and how and where they apply.

Fortunately, in commonly used services like public transport, important rules – and especially changes to rules – are usually communicated in some other way. Image 1.1 shows a poster that was displayed in London train stations in 2008.

From 1 June 2008

drinking alcohol is prohibited on public transport

Making everyone's journey more pleasant

Image 1.1 Alcohol ban

This looks very straightforward. Passengers are no longer allowed to drink alcohol on public transport. But this is not the full story. In the case of the alcohol ban, finding out what it means involves looking at the terms and conditions mentioned on the back of the Oyster card, as Transport for London's 'Terms and Conditions of Carriage' set out the details of the alcohol ban.

Example 1.2

4.5.2 Alcohol ban – on our buses and Underground trains and in our bus and Underground stations, you must not:

• consume alcohol
• be in possession of an open container of alcohol

You may be prosecuted if you disobey these requirements on our Underground trains and in our bus and Underground stations.

(Transport for London, 2012, p. 10)

Activity 1.1

Look at these lines closely. Do they include the same information as Image 1.1?

There are a number of things to consider here, not all of which are clear from the cited section. First, these conditions of carriage run to over 50 pages. Passengers are not handed a book to read before boarding public transport or when buying a ticket. As noted, however, boarding a bus and paying the fare means a traveller is nevertheless bound by these conditions. Second, the terms and conditions are not the same as the poster. While the poster makes clear that alcohol may not be consumed on public transport, the terms and conditions state that one may not be in possession of an 'open container of alcohol'. Thus, third, it is important to know what 'open container of alcohol' means; would this include a bottle of gin that had been opened but was now sealed? Fourth, finding out what 'alcohol' includes requires consulting another text, the bye-laws that regulate London transport. This is important, as lots of liquids (like perfume and mouthwash) include alcohol. Are they included in the ban? But the bye-laws do not contain this definition. Instead, they direct the reader to another text, the Licensing Act 2003, for the definition of 'alcohol'. In this case, the legal meaning and the 'common sense' meaning of 'alcohol' are the same, that is, perfume and mouthwash are not 'alcohol' for the purposes of the ban. But it is not always the case that common sense and the law coincide in this way (Slocum, 2012).

The rest of this chapter provides examples of legal language and language used in legal contexts. These examples make three things clear. First, law uses language in surprising ways; second, the way people use language can have legal consequences; and finally, looking at the language of law can help to understand language more generally.

- Legal language is not always obviously present.

Twittering away

In January 2010, much of the United Kingdom was affected by heavy snowfalls. Robin Hood Airport, near Doncaster and Sheffield, was closed, frustrating the plans of many travellers. One such person, Paul Chambers, vented his impatience on Twitter. The message that he sent to his 600 or so followers, with expletives removed, reads as follows:

Example 1.3

Crap! Robin Hood Airport is closed. You've got a week and a bit [to sort it out] otherwise I am blowing the airport sky high!

(*Chambers* v *DPP* [2012] EWHC 2157 (Admin) pgh. 12)

Activity 1.2

Consider this tweet. What is the author expressing? Is it a real threat to blow up the airport? Would a jury conclude that this is 'menacing electronic communication' and so illegal? If there had been a recent series of bombings of airports, would the tweet be read in the same way?

The author of this tweet was charged, tried and found guilty of sending a 'menacing electronic communication' (BBC News, 2012a). Under the circumstances, it would be reasonable to argue that the tweet was not a serious threat. The public reaction to Mr Chambers' conviction demonstrated that a great number of people understood that the 'threat' to blow up the airport was not a serious one, but was instead the expression of a traveller's frustration. Nevertheless, this tweet was read very literally by airport personnel, police and – at least to start with – the courts. Eventually, two years after his conviction, the High Court quashed it (BBC News, 2012b). The case is rightly seen as one relating to freedom of speech (see Green 2012), but it is also about the interpretation of language.

Whether or not something is menacing may be a question of interpretation and context. While the tweet clearly has the form associated with a threat, 'Do *x* or I'll do *y*', whether it is understood as a threat depends on how one orients to the utterance; that is, it depends on the context in which the message is placed. In relation to language, 'context' can mean any number of things, including the identity of the speaker and audience, the other language in the text, and the forum in which the text is produced. Threats are considered in detail in Chapter 3. For the moment, it is enough to notice that communication is not always straightforward. Even 'literal' language has a context that needs to be taken into account.

The six functions of language

Even if a conversation only involves two people, there are a number of other factors that need to be considered in order to understand what's going on. Indeed, the identity of the people involved in a communication can make a significant difference to the meaning of an utterance. If a known member of a 'terrorist' group made the twitter 'threat' above, it would be reasonable to construe it as a threat. Further, if the addressee of a threat is a public figure (Fraser, 1998) it is more likely to be treated seriously. How the message is communicated may also make a difference. If the message itself contains detailed demands, it is also likely to be treated as a serious threat. Thus, there are a number of factors involved in all communicative events; each factor has a function. The model introduced here comes from the work of Roman Jakobson. He argues that 'Language must be investigated in all the variety of its functions' (1960, p. 353). His model has two aspects: the first sets out the factors involved in any communicative situation; the second enumerates the functions that are attached to these factors (see Figures 1.1 and 1.2).

Figure 1.1 Factors involved in verbal communication (Jakobson, 1960, p. 353).

A brief explanation of these six factors is required before their functions can be discussed. The 'addresser' and 'addressee' are straightforward; these are the speaker (or writer) and the hearer (or reader) respectively. Of course, not all communication situations involve only two people. There may be multiple addressees, for example. The 'message' between them is what is communicated. While this looks straightforward, the message can only be understood in relation to the other factors. I will return to the message presently. The 'code' is perhaps best thought of as the language variety. Thus, the code may be English or French, 'ordinary' language or legal language. For communication to be successful, this code has to be shared. If the addresser is speaking French and the addressee is an English monolingual speaker, it makes no sense to talk about 'message'. Indeed, the lack of a common code is a recurring issue in the area of language and the law (see Chapters 4 and 6).

While Jakobson sets out his six factors in relation to verbal communication, communication may take place verbally or through a written text (or indeed using other kinds of signs; see Chapter 10). This variation can be accounted for in terms of 'contact', that is, the 'physical channel and psychological connection' (1960, p. 353) between the addresser and addressee. Finally, the 'context' is the common ground needed for communication over and above the code. For example, if a speaker starts to discuss 'that chair' while pointing to a space, it would be reasonable to expect to find the chair in the space she indicates. Co-present communication brings its own context, that is, the surrounding space. The context also refers to the immediate verbal context, the other words and phrases that occur in the utterance. In written communication, the author would have to refer to 'a chair' before 'that chair' could be invoked in any sensible way; the chair needs to be introduced as 'co-text' before it can form part of the context.

Figure 1.1 shows that while there is always an addresser and an addressee, there is a great deal which sits between them. The most obvious link between the addresser and the addressee is the message that the one 'sends' to the other. 'Send' is in scare quotes as it is important to remember that messages are not like simple objects. For example, in one sense, a cup remains a cup, regardless of how it is given or received. What the giving and receiving of the cup *means* might change; if a cup is given in the context of a prize giving ceremony, even an ordinary tea cup may be transformed into the 'winner's cup'. Nevertheless, the cup itself has not been altered. Messages aren't like cups. But there are some theories of communication which treat messages exactly like cups. For example, the conduit model of communication treats the passing of a message from one person to another as a straightforward conveyance of a thing (the message) along a simple path, a 'conduit' (Lakoff and Johnson, 1980, p. 10; Reddy, 1979). If this were an accurate model, it would be difficult to explain why people misunderstand each other, or how the tweet above can be understood by some people as a joke and by others as a threat.

To fully understand what the message is in any particular case, all six factors need to be taken into account. Moreover, the role they play in communication also needs to be considered. This is done by paying attention to their functions, as the message is common to all the functions. That is, the message is inflected with at least one of the six functions. The functions can be understood as related to one of the six factors already outlined, and so can be positioned in the same way as the factors in Figure 1.1.

```
                          REFERENTIAL
          EMOTIVE         POETIC          CONATIVE
                          PHATIC
                          METALINGUAL
```

Figure 1.2 Jakobson's six functions of language (Jakobson 1960, p. 357).

They can be arranged in this way because the functions focus on the corresponding factor. For example, if the most important thing about the message is the speaker's attitude to it (or to the addressee) the 'emotive' function is the focus. Jakobson notes that interjections are the purest expression of the emotive function of language (1960, p. 354). The 'conative' function directs focus to the addressee and is connected to wanting the addressee to do something; hence, the imperative is a form often found fulfilling this function. Performatives are also found here; these are utterances that do something by saying something (see Chapter 3).

The 'referential' function sets up relations between the message and topics or objects of discussion, like the chair in the above example. The 'phatic' and 'metalingual' functions are related to the process of communication itself. The metalingual function involves talking about talking, and is usually prominent when misunderstanding occurs. Its focus is the code; Jakobson explains: 'Whenever the addresser and/or addressee need to check up on whether they are using the same code, speech is focused on the code: it performs a *metalingual* (i.e., glossing) function' (1960, p. 356). As 'glossing' indicates, this includes defining unfamiliar terms. The phatic function, on the other hand, is related to the connection that is made between the addresser and addressee simply through talking with each other. Thus 'small talk' is a common example of phatic language. This kind of interaction is often highly ritualised (Jakobson, 1960, p. 355) and may vary according to context or culture. Phatic talk is incredibly important in establishing and maintaining not only communication but also relationships. Finally, the 'poetic' function is relevant when the focus is the message. That is, the addresser may want to communicate something through the form of the message itself. This function is usually associated with literature and poetry, however, 'Any attempt to reduce the sphere of the poetic function to poetry or to confine poetry to the poetic function would be a delusive oversimplification' (Jakobson, 1960, p. 356). All messages have a poetic function.

These functions are not mutually exclusive and in analytical terms it is important to pay attention to all of them when examining a piece of language. Instructions about how to fill in a tax return are, at first glance, the most un-poetic of all messages. However, Avery Claflin wrote a madrigal (a piece of choral music) using the text of exactly such a document. It is called 'Lament for April 15', in honour of the normal tax filing deadline in the USA. All the functions are relevant in every instance of communication (even if they appear to be absent).

While legal language might be thought to be highly referential and entirely un-poetic, some examples show that this is not the case. In the following, it should become clear that language used in a legal context and language with a legal character are both similar to and different from 'normal' language.

Activity 1.4

For all of the following examples, consider each of the six factors and corresponding functions. Some will be more relevant to the message than others, but try and examine as many aspects as possible.

Example 1.4

A person has just been arrested in the United Kingdom. At the police station, a police officer is reading the rights. She says:

You do not have to say anything, but it may harm your defence if you do not mention when questioned something which you later rely on in court. Anything you do say may be given in evidence. Do you understand?

What is the message here? What functions are the most important?

Given the addresser and where the interaction is taking place, the conative and referential functions are probably most important here. But note that the final question orients to the metalingual function, which suggests that there may not be a shared code.

Example 1.5

Lawyer: You say in your statement to police that you did not know this Mr Smith.
Witness: That is correct.
Lawyer: The video footage just seen by the court shows you and Mr Smith in a public house does it not?
Witness: Yes.
Lawyer: The video shows you having a conversation with Mr Smith?
Witness: Yeah.
Lawyer: And yet you still wish to maintain that you did not know Mr Smith?
Witness:
Lawyer: Would you like me to rephrase the question?

What is happening in this question and answer exchange? Specifically, what is the last question doing in terms of function?

Here, the referential function is important again, though it involves referring to a physical item in the immediate context, specifically, the video evidence. The length of silence is not specified but this may be relevant to how the silence is understood. Nevertheless, the last question can be understood in terms of conative function as well as being concerned with the metalingual function. Notice that the function of each utterance is influenced by what came before. The witness does not seem to have a problem with the code; so there must be another reason. The last question directs attention to this oddity; if there is no problem with the code, why has the witness not

answered the question? The reason such a question is asked is probably to do with who the real addressee of this communicative event is.
This will be considered in Chapter 5.

Example 1.6

'To every thing there is a season, and a time to every purpose under the heaven:
A time to be born, and a time to die; a time to plant, and a time to pluck up that
which is planted' (Ecclesiastes, ch 3); a time to purchase fertilizer, and a time to
take a deduction for that which is purchased. In this appeal from a Tax Court
decision, we are asked to determine when the time for taking a fertilizer deduction should be.

These are the first few lines of an American court judgment, *Schenk* v
Commissioner of Internal Revenue (686 F. 2d 315). The question to be
decided was whether pre-payment for fertiliser could be claimed
against tax in the year it was paid, rather than in the year it was spent.

The foregrounded, and perhaps unexpected, function here is the
poetic function (see Locke, 2011). The form of the opening lines, a
quote from the Old Testament, is not what would normally be
expected in a court ruling. Moreover, these particular lines will be
familiar to many people because of a song made popular by a band
called The Byrds ('Turn, Turn, Turn'). It is not obvious why these lines
have been quoted in a tax case. Is the invocation of the Bible to convey
the seriousness of the events or comment on the morality of the
conduct? Or is the judge just trying to provide some enjoyment; tax law
is not known for its entertainment value.

Exploitation of the poetic function in legal contexts is not as rare as
one might imagine. In fact, as Kleefeld notes, 'For the *brehons*, poet-
judges of ancient Ireland, the greater the gravity of the case, the more
important it was that judgment be expressed poetically' (2010, p. 22).
Indeed, formulaic language, use of alliteration and particular rhythmic
structures have a long history in the law (Tiersma, 1999, p. 100 ff.). In
legal language, the poetic function draws attention to the spoken
nature of some legal language. As such, it is often found in oaths and
other spoken rituals (see Danet and Bogoch, 1994). Consider the
following:

Example 1.7

I swear to tell the truth, the whole truth and nothing but the truth.

If it doesn't fit, you must acquit. (O.J. Simpson Trial)

I call upon these persons, here present, to witness that I, Mary Smith, do take thee, Tom Jones, to be my lawful wedded husband.

What the poetic function means depends very much on context. While for the Brehons it signalled gravity, Hobbs argues that poetic humour may be used by lawyers to downplay the weight and worthiness of a claim, thus, it is used as a persuasive technique in service of their own client (2007). But even utterances with no obvious poetry should be considered in terms of the poetic function. The lack of something in language can be just as important as the presence. (Consider the effect of a person speaking in a perfect monotone, with no change in pitch whatsoever.)

- Attention should be paid to as many aspects of a message as possible.
- Jakobson's model provides a way of identifying and specifying the most important aspects of any message.
- The language of law is not simply referential, it can even be poetic.

Axes of combination

In addition to the functions of language, attention also needs to be paid to the effects of other choices. Jakobson argues that we need to pay attention to 'the two basic modes of arrangement used in verbal behavior, *selection* and *combination*' (1960, p. 358). This means looking at the words that are used as well as paying attention to their ordering. The first is called the paradigmatic axis and the second the syntagmatic axis. Simply considering the particular words used and the word order can focus attention on how meaning is created, and communicated, one detail at a time.

The syntagmatic axis is about syntax; the word order. It is possible to describe word order in terms of subjects, verbs and objects. But when attention is being paid to the meaning of an utterance (as well as its structure) another system is useful. The following example shows the difference.

Example 1.7

1. The assailant smashed   the victim in the face.
   a. Subject   Verb   Object
   b. Actor   Process   Goal

2. The victim   was hit in the face by the assailant.
   a. Subject   Verb   Object
   b. Goal   Process   Actor

Referring to subjects, verbs and objects reveals information about the structure of a sentence, but not about what is happening in the events reported. The terminology used in 1b and 2b helps to articulate who did what to whom (Simpson, 1993). The assailant remains the 'actor' (the one doing the hitting) and the victim remains the 'goal' (the one being hit). In this model, verbs are 'processes'. Note that in the passive construction (2), the actor can be deleted.

In terms of the paradigmatic axis, consider the difference between 'hit' and 'smashed'. While both words refer to the same thing, 'smashed' suggests an action even more violent and forceful than 'hit' (Cotterill, 2004). The choices that can be made in any 'slot' in a sentence can be described in terms of the paradigmatic axis (see Example 1.8). While the syntagmatic axis can be conceived of as horizontal, the paradigmatic axis is vertical.

Example 1.8

The man   smashed   the victim   in the face.
The scoundrel hit   the target   in the face.
The aggressor thumped   the party   in the face.

The paradigmatic axis helps to see that word choices are relevant in relation to the terms which have not been chosen. 'Scoundrel', for example, is more loaded than 'man' and, while it can refer to the same person, it has a different meaning. These choices matter.

Activity 1.5

Consider the following two sentences (inspired by Hankin, 2010):

1. Mary fails to provide sustenance, food and drink to her feline.
2. The cat was deprived of nourishment, food, and drink.

What are the differences? What are the effects of these differences?

The first difference is that (1) is in the active tense and (2) is in the passive tense. As noted, one of the features of the passive tense is that agent deletion is possible. In (2) there is no agent, as the actor, Mary, has been deleted. The cat is not an actor, but the goal. Assuming that these sentences refer to the same set of real-world facts, the decisions made in constructing (2) result in Mary not being identified as the cause of the cat's hunger. The passive tense also results in a particular word order (syntagmatic axis) that allows the actor to be absent altogether. Another difference between the two sentences can be discussed in terms of the paradigmatic axis, specifically, the choice of 'feline' instead of 'cat'. 'Feline' suggests that this sentence may be from a rather more formal text than the second; it is not that common for people to refer to their pets as 'felines'.

The final detail is the use of commas. In (1), we find 'sustenance, food and drink', while in (2) we have 'nourishment, food, and drink'. Of course there is a difference (along the paradigmatic axis) between 'sustenance' and 'nourishment' but the difference in comma use is also worth paying attention to. When dealing with written language, punctuation can be crucial to meaning; compare 'Let's eat, Granddad' with 'Let's eat Granddad'. In Activity 1.5 one finds the presence and absence of what is known as the 'serial', 'list' or 'Oxford' comma. A comma after each noun, as in (2) signals a list structure, while the single comma as in (1) indicates that the second and third nouns are examples of the first. Under these rules of interpretation, (1) could be written 'sustenance, that is, food and drink'.

Hankin documents a case where the result depended exactly on the absence of the serial comma (see also Atfield, 2013). The judge insisted on the importance of this absence and ruled accordingly. Coming up with a legal argument based on the presence or absence of a comma requires considerable attention to detail. If the argument is to work, the addressees of the argument need to share (or be persuaded to share) the interpretative convention. Of course, it also relies on knowing that some authorities place great importance on the use of commas in this way.

- Every use of language involves making a choice.
- Paying attention to the choices made in any utterance helps understand the meaning.
- Even small details can make a significant difference.

Creativity

It is not necessary to look far for examples of linguistic creativity. Because each utterance requires choices along the syntagmatic and paradigmatic axis (combination and selection), every communicative act is creative. That is, while 'linguistic creativity' tends to be associated with jokes, puns and other word play, all language use is creative. Moreover, every time an utterance of any length is produced, the chances that someone else has said exactly the same thing are infinitesimally small. This is called the 'uniqueness of utterance' principle (see Coulthard, 2004).

Legal language is creative in other ways. First, legal language creates a change in the world. The change in Transport for London's terms and conditions mean that it is no longer acceptable to drink beer on a bus. It is conative, but it is also creative in that it creates a new situation and new rules of behaviour for anyone wanting to travel on their network. Second, as seen in Example 1.6, there are also some lovely examples of linguistic creativity in the law, which foreground the poetic function of language. In so far as making a legal argument requires creativity and imagination, this is not surprising.

The following example pits the creativity of advertising against the ingenuity of lawyers.

Unable to attract even a single girl, frustrated man sues Axe

Published on October 19, 2009 by Pagal Patrakar

New Delhi. In what could prove to be a major marketing and legal embarrassment for Hindustan Unilever Limited (HUL), a 26-year-old man has filed a case against the FMCG company, which owns the Axe brand of men grooming products, for 'cheating' and causing him 'mental suffering'. The plaintiff has cited his failure to attract any girl at all even though he's been using Axe products for over seven years now. Axe advertisements suggest that the products help men in instantly attracting women ...

Vaibhav claims that he had been using all the Axe products as per the company's instructions even since he first bought them. He argued that if he couldn't experience the Axe effect despite using the products as directed, either the company was making false claims or selling fake products ...

The company might argue that Vaibhav was hopelessly unattractive and unintelligent and didn't possess the bare minimum requirements for the Axe effect to take place.

'HUL might be tempted to take that line of argument, but it is very risky. There is no data to substantiate the supposition that unattractive and unintelligent men don't attract women. In fact some of the best looking women have been known to marry and date absolutely ghoulish guys. I'd suggest that the company settles this issue out of court', lawyer Ram Jhoothmalani said.

Activity 1.6

Axe advertisements (Lynx in other countries) can be found on the internet. However, note that they are rather sexist.

Thinking about how people understand advertisements, was Vaibhav Bedi justified in suing? Should advertisers only make promises they can keep?

It is not necessary to know which particular advertisements Bedi saw to make sense of the issues here. A great many 'promises' are made to consumers in the process of trying to sell them a product. The promise that Axe makes is clear from Bedi's claim. In their advertisements, a young man uses Axe and then women – often quite literally – throw themselves at him. The promise of the advertisement is obviously 'use Axe and women will find you very attractive'. Clearly this did not work for Bedi. Whether Bedi is justified in taking the company to court depends very much on how the promise of the advertisement is understood. Extravagant claims are often made for products and the audience know that these are not to be taken literally. At the same time, there are some promises that should be honoured. If a toy is advertised as being safe for children, this should be true. If a company offers a 'money back guarantee, no questions asked' it would be reasonable to think that this would be honoured.

The distinction between what really is a promise and what is not is not always clear when it comes to advertising. Telling the difference between something that is true and something that is not true is difficult in a number of contexts (Chapters 4 and 8). But the difference matters. Arguments made in relation to a complaint to the Advertising Standards Agency (ASA) in the UK provide an interesting way to think about this. The complaint was that an advertising campaign for mascara was misleading in that the models depicted had been styled with false eyelashes. The company responsible did provide a disclaimer which stated that false lash inserts had been used, in that 'small print text [in the advertisements] stated "Shot with lash inserts"' (ASA, 2010). The company's argument against the claim that the advertisement was misleading is interesting. They argued that 'the disclosed use of false lashes was a common practice in mascara ads, which consumers were familiar with, and, in and of itself, did not render the product claims or ad misleading' (ASA, 2010). That is, they argued that their audience, the target consumers, know how to tell the difference between real promises and claims that are not in fact promises when it comes to the advertising of mascara. The ASA did not agree. They found the advertisement misleading and did not allow it to run again. The 'promise' to make eyelashes appear larger is one that should be possible to keep. If it is not, one wonders what the point of mascara is.

The medium which is used to deliver a message will also have an effect on how it is understood. For example, people tend to believe what is printed in a newspaper (even though they may be aware of editorial bias). But, did it occur to you that the Axe story above is a fake? Created by Faking News (2009), it was so convincing that it was published by a number of newspapers as real news.

- The language of the law is all around us, though it is often hidden.
- Language may have legal consequences.
- To understand these consequences attention needs to be paid to the detail and the linguistic choices made.
- Like all language, the language of the law is creative.

Conclusion

The language of the law can be found in the most unexpected of places. While often hidden, it nevertheless has consequences. The omnipresence of legal language means that it makes sense for linguists to pay attention to it. When one considers the consequences that legal language can have, and the legal consequences our own utterances can have, it becomes even more obvious that the language of the law is something worth paying close attention to. Here, Jakobson's functions of language have been introduced in order to provide a framework for analysing communicative acts. The model also makes clear that all communication has a number of aspects that need to be appreciated and considered. The act of selecting particular words and combining them in particular ways can have powerful consequences; the syntagmatic and paradigmatic axes provide a good way of showing how this happens. Finally, the language of the law does not always present the face one expects. Legal language can be challenging, complex and amusing; exploring its many faces tells us not only about the world we live in but also about language itself.

2

The language of law

It should now be clear that there are different kinds of legal language. This chapter concentrates on written legal language, such as legislation and contracts. The law places a great deal of importance on written texts (Tiersma, 2001a) and these texts have particular features. This chapter begins by considering some of these features in order to see how written legal language works as well as introducing some linguistic concepts and tools that are useful in analysing these texts. It will also become clear that legal language, like the law itself, needs to be understood from a historical perspective in order to fully appreciate how it is used today (see Tiersma, 1999).

Up close and odd

Written legal language is unusual. Often called legalese, it has its own vocabulary and syntactic structure. 'It is commonly agreed to be a complex, intricate, even bizarre style of language' (Maley, 1987, p. 25).

Activity 2.1

Make a list of the kinds of features associated with 'legal language'. Do not worry about the 'proper' name for the features; perhaps start just by writing down some examples of words or phrases that seem particularly legal.

It might also help to go and find some legal language; obviously law dictionaries are good places to look for this. You might like to look at http://fuzzylaw.cardiff.ac.uk/terms, which documents lay understandings of legal terms. Susan Maret (2010) has compiled a lexicon of terms, many of which are related to the law (http://www.fas.org/sgp/library/maret.pdf). Legislation is also an excellent place to find legal language, and is widely available online.

www.bailii.org/ (UK);
www.law.cornell.edu/ (USA);
www.austlii.edu.au/ (Australia).

There are also examples of legal language in the contracts that routinely
come with mobile phones, insurance and bank accounts. These are
often given the title 'terms and conditions'.

Saying it twice

One of the most well-known features of legal language, especially
legislative language, is the use of doublets (and sometimes even
triplets), combinations of two (or three) words.

Example 2.1

- breaking and entering
- null and void
- fit and proper
- aid and abet
- goods and chattels

Activity 2.2

Consider the pairs above. Does each part of the pair mean the same
thing? Look up each of the pairs in the Oxford English Dictionary, or an
etymological dictionary. Does this suggest a reason for their pairing?

There are a number of issues to consider here, but the first has been
signalled by drawing attention to the etymology of words. After the
Norman Conquest in 1066, a great deal of French was borrowed into
English. As Crystal and Davy note, many of these terms were 'natu-
ralised' and so are not conspicuous loan words (1969, p. 209). However,
other terms borrowed from French into the legal domain have

remained more or less confined to this field. In any case, it became common to use both the English and the French term for the same concept or referent. This may have been because there was some doubt about whether the words were full synonyms; thus, it was safe to include both variants just in case there was a difference of meaning (Crystal and Davy, 1969, p. 208). In written legal language, such inclusiveness is very important. The difficulty of being exhaustive in this way is a contributing factor to the complexity of the resulting laws.

There is another explanation for the use of doublets. This relates to the poetic function of language described in Chapter 1. The pairs of words, as listed above, provide a certain rhythm. These structures suggest formality and ritual, which are important to the law (Crystal and Davy, 1969, p. 208). As already observed, this is evident in spoken legal language. Thus, a witness taking the stand in court will say:

Example 2.2

I swear to tell the truth, the whole truth and nothing but the truth.

It is not clear that there is any difference between 'the truth' and 'the whole truth'. Faced with them side by side, however, it is possible to argue that there is a difference. For example, one might argue that the 'whole truth' makes clear that 'lies of omission' are not allowed. But the formula also has a poetic function; it indicates the importance of what is happening.

Not all borrowings from French occur in doublets and finding an English version of these loans may not be possible. 'Fee simple', 'estoppel' and 'tort' all have very specific meanings in the law. The same conspicuous borrowing occurs with Latin terms. And while in some countries there has been a turn away from the use of Latin where an English version will suffice, some Latin terms are firmly entrenched. Examples of these include 'ratio decidendi', 'ex gratia', 'pro bono', 'habeas corpus' and, ironically, a number of maxims to guide the interpretation of legislation (a legal dictionary can be found at http://thelawdictionary.org/). When terms are obviously unfamiliar, they pose less of a problem. Confronted with 'ex gratia' or 'estoppel' most people will at least be aware that they do not know the meaning of the term. There are other terms, however, which are not obviously legal or unfamiliar. These include 'consideration', 'reasonable' and 'intention'. These terms are potentially very problematic as people think they know what they mean.

There is a great deal of overlap between 'ordinary' and legal language. It is important to bear this relationship is mind as it contributes to the difficulty of legal language. Even though legal language intersects in significant ways with 'normal' language, legal language can be understood as a parallel linguistic world. In what follows, legal language is treated almost as a world unto itself. To see how this works, it helps to start with individual words that populate this world.

• Legal language, like 'ordinary' language, has been influenced by history.
• For English legal language, the influence of French and Latin is notable.
• Some parts of legal language are obviously opaque, some look like 'normal' language.

The sign

The word 'sign' has a number of meanings. It can refer to a physical object in the world (see Chapter 10) or to something less tangible. This second sense, the concept of a sign, helps understand how words have meaning. While there are a number of theories that seek to make sense of such signs, foundational for linguists is Ferdinand de Saussure's definition. For de Saussure, each sign has two components, the 'signifier' and the 'signified'. The signifier is a combination of sounds. The sounds uttered when someone says 'contract' constitute the signifier. The signified is the mental concept associated with this sound string. There are two important points to make about this model. First, the sign is the *combination* of the signifier and signified; one of them by itself does not make a sign. When dealing with a sign, it is impossible to separate the signifier from the signified. The metaphor de Saussure uses is one of a piece of paper; just as it is impossible to cut just one side of a piece of paper, it is impossible to separate the signifier and signifier and still have a sign (de Saussure, 1966, p. 113).

The second point is that the link between the signifier and the signified is arbitrary. There is no reason why the sound string 'contract' is associated with the mental image of a binding legal agreement. The arbitrary connection between the signifier and the signified goes some way in understanding why 'consideration' for a non-lawyer can mean something like compassion, but for a lawyer means an essential part of a contract. In legal terms, 'consideration' is that which is given by one party when forming a contract; for example, a painter promises to paint a house in return for money. The money is the consideration; it helps turn an ordinary promise into a legal contract.

Signs acquire their meaning from the position they have relative to other signs. Thus, in de Saussure's model, signs can be understood as occupying a particular space. The space that one sign occupies cannot be taken by another sign. Thus, 'contract' means what it does because it occupies a space that is not taken up by 'writ', 'will', 'legislation' and so on. This is part of the structuralist theory of meaning.

This raises a potential difficulty with respect to the doublets encountered above. One of the reasons proposed for their form and existence is the lack of complete synonymy; it is not clear that these terms occupy exactly the same semantic space. Nevertheless, it is possible to apply the structuralist theory of meaning in three ways. This will be done with 'goods and chattels' as an example. The first way is to follow the space metaphor fully and argue that if considered as two separate signs 'goods' and 'chattels' must occupy different spaces and hence have different meanings. This focuses on the fact that 'goods' and 'chattels' have different forms; their signifiers are different. The second is to analyse the doublets as a single sign. In this analysis, the sound string 'goods and chattels' would be a signifier associated with a single signified and hence constitute a single sign.

Finally, 'goods' and 'chattels' might be treated as separate signs which, nevertheless, occupy the same space. As this contradicts what de Saussure has to say about how signs have meaning in relation to other signs, the sign space needs to be reconfigured. In the case of doublets, it would be possible to argue that the signs space is multilay-ered, with each layer representing a different linguistic origin. This would result in a kind of double occupation of the same space. This analysis is appealing as it aligns with the law's attention to definitions. Precision of meaning is important in the law. Thus, one might argue that double occupation of a sign space is a way of emphatically stipu-lating a meaning.

Definitions matter in legal writing. Legislation and contracts often include definition sections setting out the meaning of the words used.

In contractual terms and conditions, the defined terms are often capitalised. Hence, it is common to see 'the Customer' and 'the Company' in consumer contracts. Doublets can be understood as performing a similar kind of role, insisting on a meaning and marking it out at the same time. However, defining terms and insisting on particular meanings does not always make for elegant prose.

> Natural language being such a breeding ground for ambiguity, to communicate just one set of meanings while excluding many others is often impossible; but the lawyer must at least make the effort, and legal language has many oddities that are clear evidence of the kinds of effort that have been made (Crystal and Davy, 1969, p. 193).

There are some important legal terms that seem to escape definition altogether. It is possible to discuss them in terms of vagueness or ambiguity, but they do have well-established meanings; they are just not easy to define. A good example is 'reasonable'; it is 'one of the most important concepts in British and British-derived law' (Wierzbicka, 2003, p. 1). It is also a concept that has changed its meaning over time (Wierzbicka, 2003). It is found in both the criminal and civil law in collocations like 'a reasonable man', 'beyond a reasonable doubt', 'reasonable force', 'reasonable care' and 'reasonably foreseeable'. In the case of the 'reasonable man' it is possible to provide a gloss; 'an ordinary man, a humble commuter, who epitomizes an ordinary person's putatively sound judgement' (Wierzbicka, 2003, p. 1). In line with this, the concept of 'reasonable' is used when behaviour needs to be assessed as acceptable or not. For example, if a burglar breaks into a house and the occupier shoots her dead, the house owner may argue that only 'reasonable force' was being used in order to protect the property and its occupants.

What is 'reasonable' is a judgement of fact and so left to the jury (see Chapter 9). While the difficulty of defining 'reasonable' may seem to be a problem, it also allows an important space for human judgement. If every possible case of 'reasonable force' were to be included in a piece of legislation, it would run to hundreds of pages and would still not be exhaustive. While 'reasonable' may not be easy to define in other terms it does have a rather settled meaning for legal professionals. Indeed, one of the many things that lawyers acquire during their legal training is an understanding of legal language, including terms like 'reasonable'.

- de Saussure's concept of the sign provides a way of thinking about words and their meaning.
- What is a sign in legal language may not be a sign in 'ordinary language'.
- The relationship between the signifier and signified is often explicitly stated in legal texts.
- Legal language is sometimes designed to be broad and to depend on real world context.

Compounding the complexity

Long sentences are routine in written legal language. The terms and conditions of any contract will probably provide some good examples. The length is, of itself, not a problem (Owen, 1996). Issues do arise when sentence length combines with another feature common in legal language; the complex sentence. Before defining 'complex' sentences, I consider compound sentences, which are generally easy to read and understand. This is because they are comprised of a string of simple sentences joined together with words like 'and'. Consider the following example adapted from a real legal document.

Example 2.3

The patron may be allowed to remove food from the Hotel and the Hotel may allow such activity and the patron will sign an agreement and the patron will accept responsibility for the food.

This is a long sentence (34 words), but as it has a compound structure, it is easy to make sense of. It could be set out as:

Example 2.4

---

a. The patron may be allowed to remove food from the Hotel *and*
b. The Hotel may allow such activity *and*
c. The patron will sign an agreement *and*
d. The patron will accept responsibility for the food.

All the parts of the original compound sentence are vertically aligned as they are of equal importance and rank. This is the hallmark of a compound sentence.

This example includes other features typically found in written legal language. For example, the repetition of 'the patron' and 'the Hotel' makes very clear that the sentence is simply a string of shorter sentences joined together. However, this kind of repetition, using a noun instead of a pronoun (so 'the patron' instead of 's/he'), is typical of legal language. The use of pronouns for a recurrent noun phrase is called 'anaphora'. Legal texts have very low levels of pronoun use and hence low levels of anaphora of this kind. The avoidance of pronouns can assist in eliminating ambiguity; however, it is not always the most efficient way of communicating information. Nevertheless, there are some instances of anaphora in legal texts. Crystal and Davy note that 'do' and even 'this' and 'that' are commonly used in this way (1969, p. 202). In the case of compound sentences what these words refer to is easily resolved. In complex sentences, such resolution is more difficult.

Example 2.5

In the event that a patron wants to remove leftover food from the Hotel, the Hotel may allow such activity only if such patron acknowledges, by its signature below, its agreement to accept responsibility and abide by the terms set forth in this Agreement (document from a Marriot hotel in London).

This sentence is not that much longer than example 2, but it is harder to make sense of.

Activity 2.3

Set out the information in Example 2.5 in a more transparent way. Pay attention to the content and decide what the core message is.

To understand Example 2.5, it helps to split it in two. The first part sets out the situation the sentence applies to:

Example 2.6

1. The patron wants to remove leftover food from the hotel.

The rest of the sentence sets out what happens then, if 'this' is allowed to stand for (1):

Example 2.7

1. The hotel may allow this if
   a. the patron
      i. agrees to accept responsibility
      ii. and [agrees to] abide by the terms
         (1) by signing the Agreement

This is not an easy example to analyse, as the subordinate clauses (which depend on the main clause, they cannot stand alone) are themselves complex. It should also be noted that the final part, about signing the Agreement, applies to both (i) and (ii).

This sentence deals with two hypothetical scenarios. First, if the hotel allows the food to be taken, this will be acceptable if, second, the patron does what is required. While this is not a standard syntactic analysis, setting out a sentence in terms of vertical space allows the complexity to be easily seen. The representation in Example 2.7 can be a useful first step in undertaking a more technical analysis, as well as making the content easier to digest. It also captures in a visual way the difference between a compound and a complex sentence.

A compound sentence may be long, but all its component parts are equal in terms of being at the same hierarchical level; this is signalled by the level of indentation. This is not the case with the complex sentence. To make sense of, or redraft, Example 2.5, attention needs to be paid to the relationship between the clauses (the setting of the lines in Example 2.7 makes this clear).

Laying it out

While not exactly the same, modern legislation resembles Example 2.7, whereas older legislation looks a lot like Example 2.5. In recent decades, legal drafters have made much more use of layout, including numbering of subsections, for clarity of meaning and ease of navigation. In older statutes, it is not uncommon to find a block of text, with no formatting at all and very little punctuation. There are a number of theories as to why this is the case, including the idea that setting the text as a block made it more difficult to make fraudulent additions later (Crystal and Davy, 1969). The lack of punctuation may also be related to the idea that legislation was not intended to be read aloud. It has also been suggested that punctuation was not included as it was not relevant to meaning and could cause ambiguity. Indeed, while punctuation is now accepted as an interpretative aid in the UK (Slapper and Kelly, 2004, p. 203), this was not always the case.

- The component parts of a compound sentence are hierarchically equal; the parts of a complex sentence are not.
- Complex sentences are common in legal language.
- They can be harder to process than compound sentences, but their complexity can be represented visually.
- The layout of legislation has changed over time.
- Contemporary layout tends to be easier to follow.

Putting it together

The way legislation is laid out now makes it easier to follow the structure and understand its meaning. And while complex sentences are typical in written legal language, there is one complex construction that is particularly common.

Activity 2.4

This is Section 1 from The Bribery Act 2010 (UK). Look at the first three subsections. What is the basic structure underlying this? It may help to consider whether the subsections could be ordered differently.

General bribery offences
1. Offences of bribing another person
(1) A person ('P') is guilty of an offence if either of the following cases applies.
(2) Case 1 is where-
    (a) P offers, promises or gives a financial or other advantage to another person, and
    (b) P intends the advantage-
        (i) to induce a person to perform improperly a relevant function or activity, or
        (ii) to reward a person for the improper performance of such a function or activity.
(3) Case 2 is where-
    (a) P offers, promises or gives a financial or other advantage to another person, and
    (b) P knows or believes that the acceptance of the advantage would itself constitute the improper performance of a relevant function or activity.
(4) In case 1 it does not matter whether the person to whom the advantage is offered, promised or given is the same person as the person who is to perform, or has performed, the function or activity concerned.
(5) In cases 1 and 2 it does not matter whether the advantage is offered, promised or given by P directly or through a third party. (The Bribery Act 2010, s 1)

It would be possible to put subsections (2) and (3) before subsection (1). It would then have been very clear that the underlying logical structure here is:

Example 2.8

If X then Y; or
Y is true if X is true.

This structure is commonly used, not only for the description of crimes, but for other kinds of legal instructions, rights and duties.

There are of course many possible variations on this basic theme, but in nearly all of them the 'if X' component is an essential:

every action or requirement, from a legal point of view, is hedged around with, and even depends upon, a set of conditions which must be satisfied before anything at all can happen (Crystal and Davy, 1969, p. 203).

The section from The Bribery Act also highlights another significant feature of legal language. Look closely at the subsections of Section 1(2)(b). One subsection uses the words 'perform improperly' while the next chooses 'improper performance'. Note that the difference can be described in relation to the syntagmatic axis. The necessary 'adjustments', because of the chosen syntax, make clear that an action, 'performing', can also be encoded as a noun, 'performance'. While legal language tends to use a small set of verbs, it uses a large number of complex noun phrases, and can thus be said to be 'highly nominal' (Crystal and Davy, 1969, p. 205). 'Performance' is a common word, and so choosing to encode the meaning as a noun or a verb may not seem significant. But when the noun is not so common its presence does tend to be noticed. Encoding something as a noun, when it could be another kind of word (verb, adjective or adverb), is known as 'nominalisation' (Tiersma, 1999, p. 77 ff.). Attention is usually drawn to these nouns because of their final morpheme; '-ation' is particularly common. Nominalisation involves making a word into a noun. This choice can also change the perception of what is being described or referred to.

Activity 2.5

Trustee Act 2000
Section 3 General Power of Investment
(1). Subject to the provisions of this Part, a trustee may make any kind of investment that he could make if he were absolutely entitled to the assets of the trust ... . (Trustee Act 2000, s. 3)

Is there a nominalisation here? What is it? What is it doing?

The use of the noun 'investment' instead of the verb 'to invest' may not seem to be particularly important. After all, as with 'performance', 'investment' is not an unusual word. Nevertheless, it is possible to rewrite these lines as follows:

Example 2.9

General Power to Invest
1. Subject to the provisions of this Part, a trustee may invest in any way that he could if he were absolutely entitled to the assets of the trust ...

Two things change as a result of altering 'investment' to 'invest'. In this particular case, the sentence becomes shorter. One might argue that 'invest' needs a direct object (for example, 'money') but even if this were to be inserted the revised version in Example 2.9 would still be shorter than the original.

The other change is one of meaning, though not a change in reference. To 'make an investment' and 'to invest' in this context refer to the same actions. The difference between the choice of noun or verb is best described in terms of mental imagery. What kind of image does 'investment' suggest? What is this associated with? Is there any difference when compared with the image for 'invest'? 'Investment' suggests something stable, solid and tangible, especially when considered alongside its verbal counterpart. This is not due to the meaning of the root morpheme (invest) but because it is a noun. That is, nominalisations suggest that the referent, which is strictly speaking an action, is a *thing*. Thus, nominalisations suggest a kind of solid reality, a sense of something tangible, in a way that verbs do not. This is possible because language has more than one function.

According to Halliday (1985), language has three metafunctions: the textual, the interpersonal and the ideational. The textual function relates to the structure of a text, how it is constituted and thus comprehensible as a meaningful piece of language. The interpersonal acknowledges that relationships between people are affected by the use of language. Finally, the ideational metafunction relates to how language is used to make sense of the world. The ideational metafunction explains how nominalisation works. Specifically, it can be explained in terms of 'grammatical metaphor'. People tend to expect (consciously or not) that objects in the world will be referred to by nouns and actions by verbs. When this does not happen, when an action is referred to as a noun, it is a case of grammatical metaphor. Gibbons notes:

> In English, grammatical metaphor permits the dense packaging of information, particularly in the noun phrase or nominal group. This density plus the semantic mismatch between word class and meaning means that it can be difficult to understand (2001, p. 450).

At the same time, sometimes the use of grammatical metaphor simplifies syntactic structure (Gibbons, 2003, pp. 167–8). To understand the terminology it helps to remember that a metaphor expresses (and at the same time designates) a similarity. A metaphor is usually structured in the following way: '*x* is *y*'. The process that underlies nominalisation is metaphorical in the sense that it asserts an equivalence between two things that are not the same and as a result our view and understanding of that thing is changed. In the example above, an action is made into a noun, and hence a thing. The expectation that things will be referred to with nouns and actions will be described by verbs may not always be conscious, but 'It could be said that parts of speech have an "unmarked" semantics' (Gibbons, 2003, p. 19). 'Unmarked' simply means the default or neutral choice. For this reason, grammatical metaphor is also known as 'marked clause structure'.

The terminology here can be a bit misleading, in so far as saying that there is a marked and an unmarked choice suggests that the former is somehow 'neutral'. But even a 'neutral' choice conveys important information. The key point is that looking at all the possible choices makes clear that meaning always depends on what is not said.

Nominalisations are often condemned and writers are told to avoid these 'zombie words' (Sword, 2012). But they can be very useful in communicating efficiently. Similarly, writers are often advised to avoid the passive construction in favour of the active, but all forms have a purpose and a place.

- Nominalisations are common in legal language.
- Their effect can be understood with reference to the idea of grammatical metaphor.
- Nominalisation can lead to shorter and less complex sentence structure.

Searching for clarity

As Chapter 1 showed, the language of the law is everywhere, and written legal language in particular is not easy to deal with. People struggle with legal terminology when trying to understand the terms and conditions in insurance policies, they worry about their obligations under the lease they have just signed with their landlord. Contractual texts, where the audience is any consumer who happens to need insurance or a place to live, are often the object of criticism because the language is not appropriate for the communicative context.

There are a number of movements and campaigns that argue for clarity and accessibility in legal language. Collectively, this can be called the Plain English approach. Advocates for Plain English are concerned not just with legal language, but with any specialised or professional language which is not easy for lay people to understand (Clarity International; Solomon, 1996; Watson-Brown, 2012). Making written language comprehensible is important and plain language guidelines can help improve readers' understanding of texts (Kimble, 1994–5). Trying to avoid syntactic complexity, ambiguous words and unhelpful nominalisations are all important in making language more accessible to a lay reader (Gibbons, 2003, pp.166 ff.; Tiersma, 1999, pp. 211 ff.). I do not want to suggest that this is not worth doing, but there is another way of looking at the complexity found in written legal language.

Above, it was shown that signs are made up of signifiers and signifieds and that signs mean what they mean because of their relationship with other signs. I suggested above that it might be useful to see the system of legal language signs as occupying a kind of parallel world; a sign space that is related to and yet distinct from ordinary language. My point is that legal language is a language; while it relies on the basic structure of ordinary language it is highly adapted to its purpose.

Here, I want to refer to another classic linguistic theory, the Sapir–Whorf hypothesis (Lucy, 1997; Whorf, 1954). This hypothesis suggests that there is a relationship between language and worldview. There are various positions that can be taken about how strong this relationship is, with the 'strong' version often termed the 'prison house view of language'. This version states that the limits of language are the limits of thought; that if there is not a word for something, it cannot be thought. This strong version cannot be true (otherwise it would be impossible to create new words), but the Sapir–Whorf hypothesis does point out the relationship between language and thought. Halliday's grammatical metaphor and ideational metafunction of language also make connections between language and thought. In short, acquiring legal language is not limited to learning a set of terms; it is also about learning a new way of thinking, entering into a different language and a different world. I want to suggest that the parallel universe of legal signs really is a different place.

While the sign universes of legal language and normal language may be parallel they are not isomorphic, that is, they do not completely correspond.

Activity 2.7

Think about something that has a specialised terminology. It may be something related to music, dance, literature or a sports activity. Think of some of the key terms used to talk about this activity or actually do this activity. Now, think about how these terms would be 'translated' for someone who does not know anything about this area. Is it easy?

Dancers know the difference between a *jeté* and a *plié*. Musicians know the difference between a crotchet and a minim. Trying to explain these terms to someone who is not a dancer or a musician takes time. The meaning of these words is connected to the whole system of dance or music. There is not a simple single word 'translation', or even a suitable phrase, for these terms. If there was, the specialist terminology would not need to exist in the first place. In short, specialist languages construct the world, and the way users of those languages think, in very particular ways. Accounts of Plain English do take this into consideration. For example, guidelines from Queensland, Australia note:

> Plain English does not involve the simplification of a law to the point it becomes legally uncertain. In particular, care needs to be taken that legal uncertainty is not created when dispensing with terms having established meanings for users of legislation. Plain English may involve a balance of simplicity and legal certainty to ensure the law is both easily read and understood and legally effective to achieve the desired policy objectives.
>
> (Queensland Government, 2011, section 3.5.1)

I am not suggesting that it is impossible to construct texts that both serve a legal purpose and allow for lay understanding. Nor am I suggesting that making legal texts accessible is a bad idea. But it is worth bearing in mind that legal language is, to some extent at least, a different language. Thus, the construction of a good Plain English 'translation' requires input from legal professionals who are highly literate in both legal and lay language; it requires the participation of willing bilingual professionals (Tiersma, 2001b). Ultimately, what is required is that legal texts are written in plain language from the start as then translation would not be needed (Kimble, 1994–5, p. 55). This, however, will take time simply because a great many legal texts still in force were composed some time ago.

- Legal language may be the most effective and comprehensible variety if the addressee is a legal professional.
- Plain English is highly desirable for texts addressed to a lay audience.
- The move from 'legal English' to 'Plain English' is akin to a translation.
- Because of this, the move to Plain English requires the involvement of willing legal professionals who are bilingual.

Conclusion

Written legal language typically includes specialised terminology, complex sentences, high levels of nominalisation and low levels of anaphora. People often say legal language is difficult to understand; it is called 'jargon' or 'legalese'. However, legal language is entirely appropriate, and indeed required, in certain situations. The problem arises when legal language is used to address an audience, or for a purpose, for which it is not suited. Legal language is an efficient, clear and suitable mode for legal professionals to talk to each other, but it is baffling for anyone not fluent in the law. Needless to say, this is true of all specialised languages and terminologies, whether medical language, philosophical discourse or plumbing terminology. The problem is that legal language has consequences for everyone.

3
Don't do it!

As Chapter 1 showed, language has a number of functions. This chapter deals with two specific things that language can be used to do: threaten and warn. These have been chosen for two reasons. First, threats and warnings have a great deal in common and it is not always easy to distinguish between a threat and a warning. Second, they show different aspects of the law. While it is (in some cases) illegal to make threats, warnings are required for a number of consumer products. Thus, while some threats are illegal, many warnings are legally required.

Read this!

While the law may punish people for committing acts, it can also hold people to account for not doing something. In the case of some dangers, there is a legal duty to warn people. This is certainly the case with respect to consumer goods. Many things that people use on a daily basis have risks attached to them. But avoiding danger may only be possible if the consumer knows what the danger is. While warnings can be delivered using a specific verb, such as 'I warn you' or 'I advise you', in the case of consumer products they are very often included under headings like 'information', 'caution' and 'instructions'.

For warnings to work they need to be clear. As warnings may address large and diverse audiences, they need to be written simply, in an accessible language and style (Tiersma, 2002). Warnings need to be adequate in terms of the information they communicate and the language used to do this (Tiersma, 2002). When establishing exactly which features will be relevant to adequacy it helps to consider what a warning is trying to do. A warning is generally for the benefit of the hearer. As the addressee may control the outcome (whether the bad thing happens or not) logically, the receiver of the warning needs to know what the danger is and how to avoid it. Informing someone of a risk should also explain why it is a risk. Further, warnings 'should not be too weak or indirect' (Tiersma, 2002, p. 57). Thus a warning should state:

1. What the danger is
2. How to avoid it
3. Why it should be avoided
4. What to do if harm occurs (adapted from Shuy, 1998, p. 171 cited in Tiersma, 2002, p. 64).

Activity 3.1

You buy a cup of coffee from a take-away coffee shop. While you are taking the lid off to put sugar in, you spill the coffee over your stomach. You suffer third degree burns; you require skin grafts and two weeks in hospital. When you complain to the shop, they point out some text on the side of their cups which reads 'CAUTION: CONTENTS HOT!' Is this an adequate warning?

The message on this cup of coffee is not one with a great many words. Nevertheless, its adequacy can be assessed by paying attention to the four features of an adequate warning. This warning does not say what the danger is, nor does it state how to avoid the risk, why it should be avoided or what to do if the unspecified risk is encountered. All four components of the warning need to be inferred. Some of these inferences are straightforward, some less so.

Although there is not much text, if attention is paid to the paradigmatic axis, the warning can be further analysed. This warning is presented not as a 'warning' but as a 'caution'. An understanding of how signs have meaning (Chapter 2) suggests that a 'caution' is less forceful than a 'warning'. Nevertheless, it indicates that there is some risk. The description of the contents as 'hot' in the main body of the warning allows the danger to be inferred. Hot things burn. But people expect coffee to be hot. Thus, one might conclude that this is not really a warning.

If it is a warning, it is possible to infer that 'hot' suggests the risk of burning the inside of the mouth. This is common-sense; people do not consume hot drinks in the same way as cold ones. But while a burnt mouth is hardly pleasant, it is not a serious risk. The danger all depends on how 'hot' is understood. Again, the theory of how signs have meaning and consideration of the paradigmatic axis suggest that while 'hot' is warmer than 'cool', it is less warm than 'very hot' or 'boiling'. In the light of the consequences described in Activity 3.1, this is not an adequate warning. If the heat of a liquid is such that it causes third degree burns it is clearly warmer than 'hot'. Certainly coffee should be hot, it may even be 'very hot', but the 'scalding' nature of this cup of coffee is not easily inferable from the warning provided.

This example is based on an American lawsuit against McDonald's (*Liebeck* v *McDonald's*; see Cain 2007, *Hot Coffee* 2011). While the case is often used to argue that there has been an increase in frivolous lawsuits (Chapter 9), the information about the degree of burns suffered is not usually mentioned.

Activity 3.2

Find the packaging for a medicine in your house. It does not need to be something that is prescribed, a box of painkillers will do. See if there are any warnings on the box or inside. Remember that warnings are sometimes included in 'instructions'. What form do the sentences take? What kinds of words are used? Are there any pictures or icons? Where is the text? Is the warning adequate?

Looking at the four features of an adequate warning, it might seem that they could be presented to a reader in any order at all. If a warning is contained in a series of short bullet points, the order probably does not matter that much. But as inserts in medicine make clear, some warnings are quite long. In such cases, the order in which the information is given can be crucial to the adequacy of the warning.

Imagine the following text on a packet of over-the-counter medication for hay fever (inspired by Shuy, 1990):

Example 3.1

(1) Strokes can occur at any time. (2) They can be fatal if early intervention does not take place. (3) If you experience any symptoms of a stroke, you should

immediately seek medical assistance. (4) This medication has a new chemical ingredient. (5) Tests conducted suggest that this ingredient may lead to blood clotting.

Activity 3.3

Is this a good warning? Why not? Is there a better way of ordering this information?

As all the features in Example 3.1 contain information, they can be considered to be 'information chunks'. In order to analyse longer warnings, it can help to classify these chunks (generally a sentence or a main clause) according to the four features of an adequate warning. This will reveal whether information is presented in a logical order. In terms of the four features of an adequate warning, it is easy to see that there are some parts that should be placed before others. For example, it makes sense to be told what the danger is before being told how to avoid it. More generally, a good principle of textual structure is for the most important information to be placed near the start (Shuy, 1990). This helps to make the 'logic' and 'argument' of the text clear and in turn makes the text more comprehensible. A warning may contain all the necessary elements, but if they are not ordered in a logical way, the text will probably not be very informative.

Inferences need to be made when the connection between two chunks, or the reason for the presence of a chunk, is not clear or explicit. An informative text is one which minimises the number of inferences that the reader needs to make as readers have to infer less when information is logically structured. For informative texts, like warnings, a logical structure is one that provides 'given' information before 'new' information. 'Given' information, as the name suggests, is anything that the reader should already know, either from the text that came before or from immediate context.

Shuy points out that in warnings the association between the danger and the activity should be easy to access, that is, it should be easy to infer. Given that the warning in Example 3.1 is on a packet of medication for hay fever, it is not clear why strokes are mentioned at all in (1); it is a difficult inference to generate. Sentence (4) would be a better place to start, as it relates directly with the product at hand, 'this medication'. The medicine is 'given', the reader has it in her hand, while the 'new ingredient' is new information. Moving these chunks around so that the 'new' in one sentence can function easily as 'given' in the next results in the following:

Example 3.2

(4) This medication has a new chemical ingredient. (5) Tests conducted suggest that this ingredient may lead to blood clotting. (1) Strokes can occur at any time. (2) They can be fatal if early intervention does not take place. (3) If you experience any symptoms of a stroke, you should immediately seek medical assistance.

This is better, but the link between 'blood clotting' and a stroke still needs to be inferred. There is also no information about the symptoms of a stroke. Nevertheless, simply reordering information chunks can make a difference to the comprehensibility of a text. Paying attention to textual structure and assessing what can easily be inferred are good ways of evaluating whether warnings are adequate. Further, in some jurisdictions, it is permissible to ask members of the public how they understand a particular warning. This can then be used in arguments relating to the adequacy of the warning in question (Johnson, 1990).

- Informative texts should be structured in a certain way.
- They should not cause the reader to have to infer important information.
- There are four elements of a good warning; while some may be easy to infer from the context, they should all be easily accessible to a wide range of readers.

Doing things with words: speech acts

The written warnings considered so far are clearly trying to communicate information. But they are also doing something else.

> ### Activity 3.4
>
> Look at the statements below. Who would say them and in what context?
> Do they have any consequences?
>
> a. I'm telling you, don't do it!
> b. Stop before it's too late.
> c. I now pronounce you man and wife.
> d. It is the judgment of this court that the defendant, John Smith, shall
>   be and hereby is sentenced to a term of imprisonment of 150 years.
> e. Guilty.

In (a) the speaker is not just 'telling' someone something, she is ordering or advising. In (b), the speaker is warning, or perhaps threatening, or even pleading. In (c) the speaker is not simply saying something; she is marrying a woman and man. The consequences of (d) are that John Smith will stay in jail for rather a long time. The example in (e) requires a bit more context. In jury trials, the judge will ask whether the jury has reached a verdict, if they have, she will then ask the foreperson to give that verdict. Thus, as an answer to the judge's question, one word is enough to 'find' or 'pronounce' the defendant 'guilty'. Note that the judge already knows the verdict. The question from the judge is, in that sense, not a 'real' question. The whole exchange is an official and legal performance; it is also a speech act.

The examples in Activity 3.4 all *do* something. However, they only do something if other conditions are in place. (Unless you are qualified to do so, saying (c) to a couple will have no legal effect on them whatsoever). It also makes no sense to say they are 'true' or 'false'. While it is possible to assess the truth of the statement 'the robbery took place during the night' it does not make sense to say 'I now pronounce you man and wife' is true (or false). The person pronounced 'Guilty' in (e) may well be innocent; the fact of his guilt may be in dispute. But it is impossible to say 'We find the defendant guilty' is either true or false.

In his speech act theory, Austin distinguishes between constatives (which can be true or false) and performatives (which cannot).

I want to discuss a kind of utterance which looks like a statement ... and yet is not true or false ... in the first person singular present indicative active ... if a person makes an utterance of this sort we would say that he is *doing* something rather than merely *saying* something ... When I say *I do* (take this woman to be lawful wedded wife), I am not reporting on a marriage, I am indulging in it (Austin, 1979, p. 235).

Moving away from a view of language which prioritises truth claims, Austin realised that understanding language involves more than assessing factual evidence or syntactic acceptability. Speech Act Theory is an important concept when looking at language in a legal context. First, it helps understand why some speech acts have legal effects. Second, it is important in understanding why some speech acts are illegal. In fact, in his book, *How To Do Things With Words*, Austin often refers to the legal context. As such, there is a long association between legal language and speech act theory.

Activity 3.5

Consider the following examples:

a. A police officer stops a person going into her place of work, saying 'Don't go in there'.
b. At a swimming lake, a park ranger says 'I have to warn you that the lake is very shallow today; it's not a good idea to jump off those rocks'.
c. A person goes up to a bank teller and places a gun on the counter saying 'give me the money'.

Describe these utterances. What do they do?

In all of the examples here, the spoken words have simply been reported by using the verb 'to say'. But they are all doing more than simply saying. The police officer in (a) is saying something, but she is also ordering. Even though it is an indirect speech act (she does not use the verb 'order') it is still clearly an order. She may also be warning, either about the consequences of disobeying or that there is something unpleasant inside. Finally, this may have some other kind of effect. It may cause the addressee to be frightened.

There are a number of ways of identifying and naming speech acts. Sometimes an explicit performative is used, that is, a verb which announces the action that is being undertaken. In the example above, the park ranger uses the verb 'warn' in her warning speech act; it is a direct speech act. In some legal contexts, the performative verb is clearly foregrounded:

Example 3.4

Be it enacted by the Queen's Most Excellent Majesty, by and with the advice and consent of the Lords Spiritual and Temporal, and the Commons, in this present Parliament assembled, and by the authority of the same, as follows:

Example 3.5

I hereby swear that the following statements are true.

In Example 3.4, the performative verb is placed at the front of the sentence. The action being performed is the enacting of a piece of legislation. In Example 3.5, the performative verb 'swear' is pre-modified by 'hereby'. As Austin notes, words like 'hereby' are common in performatives and are a clear indication that a speech act is present (1980, pp. 57–8). As the examples in Activity 3.5 show, though, it is not always the case that a performative verb is used. The police officer in activity 3.5 (a) above simply uses the imperative form of the verb; and while this is a common form for issuing orders, there is no explicit performative verb.

The second way to know which speech act is being performed is to think of how the utterance would be reported to someone else. Would it be reported in terms of simple speech 'she said' or rather some other way, for example, 'she insulted me'. Not all speech acts have a corresponding performative verb. It is not possible to say 'I hereby insult you', but that does not mean that insults are not speech acts. It simply means that some other form of words must be used to deliver the insult. The three different kinds of acts that Austin identifies help understand this.

1. Locutionary acts
2. Illocutionary acts
3. Perlocutionary acts

Locutionary acts are those where the doing is the saying; that is, the speech act is 'saying'. Even straightforward declaratives (which are true or false) are locutionary acts. An illocutionary act is performed when something more than saying takes place; a speech act is performed *in* the saying. Typical examples of illocutionary acts include promises, apologies, requests and orders. Saying 'I promise' is to make the promise; the saying is the doing. As noted, some illocutionary acts can be performed by using the appropriative performative verb; 'I order you to do it now' is obviously an order.

Finally, perlocutionary acts go one step further. They perform an act *by* saying something. Examples of perlocutionary acts include persuading, convincing, insulting and deceiving. It is not possible to persuade someone by using a particular performative verb. One cannot say 'I hereby persuade you' in the way that one can say 'I hereby promise you'. Perlocutionary acts are the result of locutionary and illocutionary acts. For example, it is possible to persuade someone to go to a concert with you by promising to buy her something. While it is important to distinguish between locution, illocution and perlocution, they are also related to each other. Thus, every illocutionary act necessarily involves a locutionary act too; it is not possible to verbally threaten someone without saying something. Likewise, it is not possible to verbally convince someone without performing some illocutionary (and hence also locutionary) acts; for example, challenging, demonstrating or reporting. Thus, a perlocutionary act entails an illocutionary act, and an illocutionary act entails a locutionary act. But it is not the case that every locution is also an illocution (or a perlocution).

- Speech acts do things with words.
- There are three different kinds of speech acts; locutionary, illocutionary and perlocutionary.
- Illocutionary and perlocutionary acts cannot be true or false.
- An illocutionary speech act may or may not use a performative verb.

Happy yet?

While declaratives may be assessed on the basis of whether they are true and false, speech acts are assessed on the basis of 'felicity conditions'. Because of the etymology of 'felicity' (from the Latin 'felix' meaning happy), speech acts can be 'happy' (when felicity conditions are met) or 'unhappy' (when they are not).

Austin's account of felicity conditions allows consideration of the conventions involved in illocutionary acts (like marriages), the kind of people involved, and their intentions and subsequent conduct. (Note that perlocutionary acts do not have these conventions.)

> A. (i) There must exist an accepted conventional procedure having a conventional effect, that procedure to include the uttering of certain words by certain persons in certain circumstances, and further,
> (ii) the particular persons and circumstances in the given case must be appropriate for the invocation of the particular procedure invoked.
> B. (i) The procedure must be executed by all participants both correctly and
> (ii) completely
> C. (i) Where, as often, the procedure is designed for use by persons having certain thoughts or feelings or for the inauguration of certain consequential conduct on the part of any participant, then a person participating in and so invoking the procedure must in fact have those thoughts or feelings, and the participants must intend so to conduct themselves, and further
> (ii) must actually so conduct themselves subsequently.
>
> (Austin, 1980, pp.14–15)

Austin argues that if A–B are not met, the speech act 'misfires', whereas if C is not met, an 'abuse' of the speech act has taken place. In the latter case, the speech act has still been performed. (It is important to note that Austin did not see this list as being exhaustive.)

For particular cases, the terms to describe the failed speech act may be less important than identifying exactly what is lacking. In any case, once the lack has been discovered, giving it a label in Austin's terms is straightforward. In a legal or official context, cases can be more or less clear cut. Very formal illocutionary acts, for example, generally stipulate who can perform the act as well as setting out the particular form of words to be used. A good example of how seriously this is taken is President Obama's first swearing in to office. He was being sworn in by Chief Justice Roberts.

Example 3.6

The Constitution of the United States of America provides the wording for the Presidential oath of office: 'I do solemnly swear (or affirm) that I will faithfully execute the Office of President of the United States, and will to the best of my Ability, preserve, protect and defend the Constitution of the United States' (Article 2, section 1: Bill of Rights Institute). When President Obama was first sworn into office, the following occurred:

Roberts: I, Barack Hussein Obama …
Obama: I, Barack …
Roberts: … do solemnly swear …
Obama: I, Barack Hussein Obama, do solemnly swear …
Roberts: … that I will … execute the Office of President to the United States faithfully …
Obama: … that I will execute …?
Roberts: … the Off … faithfully the Pres … the Office of President of the United States …
Obama: … the Office of President of the United States faithfully …
Roberts: … and will to the best of my ability …
Obama: … and will to the best of my ability …
Roberts: … preserve, protect and defend the Constitution of the United States.
Obama: … preserve, protect and defend the Constitution of the United States.
Roberts: So help you God?
Obama: So help me God.
Roberts: Congratulations, Mr. President. Very best wishes (Obama, 2009)

Because the swearing into office is so important, and to ensure that questions would not be raised about the legitimacy of this speech act, there was a second oath taken the following day (CNN Politics, 2009). In this instance there was no question about the intention of the parties or their subsequent conduct. But this is not always the case.

Did you mean it?

Intention seems straightforward until real events are considered. While people are generally sure of their own intentions, it is not always possible to know what is in the minds of other people. In relation to speech acts, there are at least two things which might be called 'intention'.

1. Intention to commit a particular speech act (e.g. intending to make a promise).
2. Intention to do something over and above the speech act (e.g. intending to honour the promise).

Both of these seem to fall under Austin's C(i) condition above. The person performing the speech act must 'in fact' have the thoughts and feelings their speech act indicates and she must actually intend to conduct herself in the way indicated by the speech act. The proof of (2) is captured by Austin's C(i) if the intention is to do something like frighten or persuade, and in C(ii) if particular actions need to be taken. However, given that many speech acts are conventional (see Austin's A and B above), a speaker might follow the procedure and yet argue that she did not have the requisite intention. If someone says 'I'm sorry', it is still possible to argue that she did not mean it. Further, some speech acts are only more or less conventional; consider the twitter 'threat' encountered in Chapter 1 (see also BBC, 2012a).

While this makes intention more complicated, it does not really solve the problem of discovering an individual's intention. Austin's model does not provide a way of determining if the speaker in fact has the necessary thoughts and feelings. This is simply because no model can predict whether people actually mean what they say. At the moment of the speech act, all that can be relied on are the words used and anything that can be observed in the speaker's general conduct. It is worth noting that Austin did not seem to be particularly concerned with either intention or sincerity, though he did allow that they were worthy of discussion.

Activity 3.6

In UK law, Section 4 of The Offences Against the Person Act 1861 (as amended by Criminal Law Act 1977) reads as follows:

Whoever shall solicit, encourage, persuade or endeavour to persuade, or shall propose any person to murder any other person, whether he be a subject of her Majesty or not, or whether he be within the Queen's Dominions or not, shall be guilty of a misdemeanour, and being convicted shall be liable to imprisonment for life (Offences Against the Person Act 1861, s. 4).

In 2004, a satirical media commentator, Charlie Brooker, wrote a piece in a newspaper supplement expressing the hope that a particular American Presidential candidate would not be elected. The final line of the piece named some infamous assassins of former American Presidents concluding, 'where are you now that we need you?' (Steyn, 2004).
   Would this fall under section 4? Is Brooker encouraging murder?

The newspaper thought there was potentially a problem and published an apology, noting that, 'Although flippant and tasteless, his [Brooker's] closing comments were intended as an ironic joke, not as a call to action – an intention he believed regular readers of his humorous column would understand' (Guardian, 2004). The apology makes sense in terms of section 4, as the law does not require anyone to actually be persuaded; it only requires that a speaker can be understood as trying to persuade. Persuasion is a perlocutionary act, something which is not conventionally done. Thus, while it may be possible to empirically test whether someone was persuaded, arguing that persuasion was intended is rather more difficult.

   Because of the difficulty of measuring or even discerning intention (over and above what is on the face of someone's speech act), some researchers have focused on how the speech act is understood. This involves looking at 'uptake', that is, how speech acts are received. I deal with this below.

- For a speech act to be happy, certain felicity conditions need to be met.
- If conventions are clear, it may be easy to assess whether a speech act is happy.
- Intention is problematic if defined in relation to the speaker's real state of mind.

Is that a promise or a threat?

Threats and warnings are often treated together as in many respects they are similar. Further, they are both related to promises as they all orient to future actions. Threats and promises are similar in that they both indicate something about the future intentions of the speaker (see also Shuy, 1993, p. 98).

Table 3.1 Threats and warnings: similarities and differences

The act is oriented	Threat	Warning	Promise
To the speaker's benefit	No	No	No
To the addressee's benefit	No	Yes	Yes
To the speaker's detriment	No	No	No
To the addressee's detriment	Yes	No	No
Speaker controls outcome	Yes	?	Yes
Addressee controls outcome	?	?	?
Speaker committed to act	No	No	Yes

Source: Fraser (1998, p. 166)

The similarities and differences can be set out according to the various orientations of these speech acts (Table 3.1).

Fraser includes 'to the speaker's detriment' even though none of the speech acts he covers seem to be to the detriment of the speaker. It is a useful inclusion, however, as it invites consideration of the possibility that a promise, for example, may be detrimental to the speaker (even though this is not indicated in the table). Fraser also includes '?' in some categories, indicating that sometimes the answer will be 'yes' and sometimes 'no'. For example, a warning about bad weather does not relate to something within a speaker's control; it is nevertheless a warning (Fraser, 1998, p. 164).

The issue of 'intention' is arguably captured in Fraser's 'commitment to act'. How the addressee can know of such a commitment is still problematic and it is possible to look at the effect of a speech act in order to make a decision about intention. Storey (1995), for example, argues that for a threat to be a threat it has to be received as such by the hearer. If Peter threatens to cut Mary's hair but she would actually quite like for her hair to be cut, Storey's model would say it is not a threat. This model emphasises the addressee's state of mind.

Fraser's work on threats takes a different approach, as he focuses on the intention of the speaker. It is an elegant and robust definition. He sets out three components to define the act of threatening.

C1 The speaker's intention to personally commit an act (or be responsible for bringing about the commission of the act);
C2 The speaker's belief that this act will result in an unfavourable state of the world for the addressee;

C3 the speaker's intention to intimidate the addressee through the addressee's awareness of the intention in C1 (1998, p. 161).

While C1 and C2 are necessary for a threat, they are not enough without C3. Thus, if all three conditions are satisfied, a 'successful' threat has been made. Note that there is nothing here about the person being threatened as: 'a threat is successful independent of the addressee's beliefs' (Fraser, 1998, p. 162). For a threat to be communicated, the addressee has to recognise the speaker's intentions (C1 and C3) and the speaker's belief (C2). The addressee may not be intimidated, even though the threat has been communicated; she may not agree that the threatened state of affairs is to her detriment, for example.

A successful threat is not the same as a felicitous threat. This requires three additional things. First, the speaker must believe she can perform the action she has proposed; the action should be something under her control. This is often to do with power. Thus, an inferior can perform a successful threat by threatening to fire her boss, but as this is not within her control it is infelicitous (1998, p. 163). Second, in the case of a conditional threat ('if you don't do x I will do y'), a felicitous threat also requires that it is possible for the hearer to satisfy the condition. Finally, again in the case of a conditional threat, the speaker must want the condition to be met.

Thus, there are three sets of conditions that can be satisfied. The threat can be successful or unsuccessful; this relies on the speaker's intentions and beliefs. The threat can be happy or unhappy; this depends on the speaker's beliefs and abilities. The threat can be communicated or not; this relates to whether the addressee recognises the speaker's intentions. Fraser thus provides a detailed definition of threats which takes account of the variables of intention and uptake. However, he notes that while it is possible to define a threat 'it is virtually impossible ... to determine with certainty when a threat has been made' (1998, p. 162).

More than words

Activity 3.7

Consider the following scenario. You are in a country where the police carry guns. You are driving and you are stopped by two police officers. With a hand resting on their holster, one of them says 'Please step out of the car'. What kind of speech act is this?

While this looks like a straightforward request, there may be serious consequences for not complying. Philip Shon has examined exactly this question (2005). He argues that because of the authority police have and the weapons they carry, what looks like a request from an officer is far more than this. At the very least it is a warning, and it may even be a threat. Because the officer carries a gun, there is a constant underlying possibility that the firearm will be used. (Note that this account does not claim that the police officers intend to threaten members of the public.) It is possible to see the same kind of effect in any encounter involving an implicit threat of force. A 'polite' request from an armed mugger will still be reported as a threat. Shon gives a nice example. If an armed robber says 'May I please have all of your money?' the threat relies not on the language but 'on the performative effects of a gun' (2005, p. 841). Other things can have performative effects; someone standing too close or even someone in a position of authority will change the way utterances are understood. These are all connected to some of Fraser's features (Fraser, 1998, p. 170). Specifically, they relate to the speaker's intent to intimidate and the hearer's recognition of this.

It is important to note that linguistic definitions of threats do not necessarily map directly on to threats that the law would want to punish or prevent. Further, while the law, like linguistics, is concerned with intention, it has its own model which does not always rely on finding out what someone actually thought or intended. Nevertheless, being able to distinguish the fine detail of speech acts in a linguistic sense can be useful in addressing legal criteria.

- Threats, warnings and promises are closely related.
- Distinguishing between them requires close attention to the interests and intentions of the speaker and the addressee.

- While definitions of speech acts can be precise, speech acts are not always easy to identify.
- Whether something is actually heard as a serious threat depends on a number of other circumstances, not just on the language used.

What is it?

Warnings have to be adequate; they have to be comprehensible in order to protect the manufacturer or retailer from lawsuits. The act of warning is required. On the other hand, some speech acts are not legal. The distinction between speech that is just speech and speech that is labelled an 'action' is important. This may be particularly true in countries with strong freedom of speech protections. In the United States, for example, the First Amendment (to the Constitution, see Example 3.7) provides the basis for what has been held to be a very broad protection of speech.

Example 3.7

Congress shall make no law respecting an establishment of religion, or prohibiting the free exercise thereof; or abridging the freedom of speech, or of the press; or the right of the people peaceably to assemble, and to petition the Government for a redress of grievances.

As speech is protected, whether something is allowed may depend on whether an utterance is construed as 'speech' or as an 'act'. The case of *Snyder* v *Phelps et al.* (562, US, 2011), which went all the way to US Supreme Court, provides a good illustration of this. A religious group, unhappy with many aspects of American political policy, routinely mounts protests at funerals. As they are unhappy about the presence of homosexuals in the military, they often protest at military funerals (regardless of the sexuality of the deceased). In the Snyder case, the protestors had let local police know they would be protesting, and they kept to public land near, but not adjacent to, the church in which the funeral was being held. The majority of the Court held that the protest was on a topic of public, rather than private, concern and thus was protected by the First Amendment; the protest was understood as 'speech'. Mention was also made of the fact that the protestors 'honestly believed' what they were saying.

The importance of the distinction between speech and action can be seen in the way the protest is described by the judges. Those who held the protest was protected by law described the writing shown on signs carried during the protests as 'statements', 'signs', 'messages', 'views', 'speech', 'picketing' and so on. One judge, Justice Alito, did not agree and called the protest a 'vicious verbal assault'. Thus, he describes the event as an act; an 'assault'.

Even in countries without the freedom of speech rules found in the US, some kinds of speech are usually forbidden by proscribing the (speech) *act*. By happy coincidence, such naming is itself a speech act, very often taking the form of legislation. Thus, language (legislation) performs an act (making a law) which changes some kinds of speech (as well as other communicative acts) into illegal acts.

- What is speech and what is an 'action' may be defined by law.
- This difference may be defined and declared by a legal speech act.

Conclusion

Whether they are threats, warnings or pieces of legislation, speech acts are important. While defining a particular speech act is possible, this requires consideration of a number of factors. Identifying speech acts in the world, however, is not straightforward. The features considered – intention, uptake and context – may need to be carefully specified and defined for this identification to take place. Because of the different goals that linguistics and the law have, there are often differences when it comes to the definition and importance of these features. Nevertheless, linguistic terms of analysis provide an excellent way of identifying the issues that need to be addressed in legal contexts.

4

That's not what I meant!

This chapter deals with Grice's Co-operative Principle and the related conversational maxims. This model helps to understand how communication works and how people conventionally use forms of words to communicate something other than what the words literally mean. Grice's work makes clear that there is a difference between the meaning (the words spoken) and the message (how they are understood). This difference can be accounted for in terms of 'implicature'. As this is sometimes called 'pragmatic presupposition', it needs to be distinguished from 'semantic presupposition', also known as presupposition. The legal examples used in this chapter show that even though legal conversations might seem very different from normal conversations, they rely on many of the same communicative conventions. At the same time, the law has its own conventions which dictate how utterances are understood.

Activity 4.1

Your friend Sally is talking about a mutual acquaintance, Bernard.

'I'm not saying Bernard is a liar, but don't you think it's strange that he said he was there but no-one remembers seeing him?'

Is Sally saying that Bernard is lying?

Even though Sally has explicitly said that she is not claiming Bernard is a liar, she is certainly suggesting it. The explicit denial at the start might be used to argue that Sally is not accusing Bernard of lying; but that is not how her words would normally be understood. Siegel (2005) argues that the different interpretations have to do with the amount of attention people give an utterance. That is, in a normal conversation, everyone will understand that Sally is calling Bernard a liar. If, however, the written texts are examined, it is more likely that the interpretation will be the opposite. The disclaimer at the start seems to be taken more literally if there is time to examine it. Of course, this second scenario – paying close attention to the written text – is much more like jury deliberation than hearing the exchange as a casual bystander. The difference matters, because in some countries, saying something that damages a person's reputation may result in a lawsuit.

Activity 4.2

Consider the following question and answer sequence.

Police officer: Did you take part in the robbery?
Suspect: I wasn't even near the bank on John Street!

What is the suspect communicating?

It is easy to see that the answer the suspect gives is a denial, even though she does not actually say 'no'. This kind of meaning can be accounted for by H.P. Grice's Co-operative Principle (CP) and its four associated maxims. Depending on what information had already been given to the suspect, the identification of a particular bank might also be relevant. This can be described in terms of 'given' and 'new' (see Chapter 3). If the topic had already been introduced by the police, it is 'given' and so of no consequence. But if it is 'new' the police officer would probably ask some follow-up questions. Notice that the suspect also indicates that there is a bank on John Street. She does not put the fact in exactly that way; rather, something like 'there is a bank on John Street' is embedded in her utterance. This is a presupposition. I start with Grice before moving on to presupposition.

Grice defines the CP as follows:

Make your conversational contribution what is required, at the stage at which it occurs, by the accepted purpose or direction of the talk exchange in which you are engaged. (1989, p. 26)

The CP has four maxims.

1. Quantity – 'make your contribution as informative as is required (for the current purposes of the exchange)' and 'do not make your contribution more informative than is required'.
2. Quality – 'Do not say what you believe to be false' and 'Do not say that for which you lack adequate evidence'.
3. Manner – 'Avoid obscurity of expression', 'Avoid ambiguity'; 'Be brief' and 'Be orderly'.
4. Relevance – 'Be relevant' (Grice, 1989, pp. 26–7).

Some scholars argue that all the maxims can be contained under the fourth, relevance (Sperber and Wilson, 1986). It helps to have the four maxims, though, as they can assist in directing attention to specific aspects of an utterance.

There is often some confusion over Grice's Co-operative Principle and it is a good idea to deal with this at the outset. The word 'co-operative' may suggest that Grice is saying something about what speakers *should* do. That is, it is tempting to think that for a conversation to work the maxims have to be obeyed. This is not Grice's claim. Consider the interaction between the police officer and the suspect in Activity 4.2. The most helpful and informative answer that the suspect could have given would have been a 'yes' or 'no'. As she did not do this, she has 'flouted' one of the maxims. Flouting a maxim is very common and it leads to an 'implicature'. The implicature here is that she was not involved in the robbery. But note that she did not actually *say* this. Rather, through the operation of flouting and the resulting implicature, she *communicated* it. In a sense, the maxims are obeyed overall in that what looks like an uncooperative contribution is saved by the operation of implicature. The implicature is generated to make the contribution meaningful.

The CP makes no claims about what speakers do or what they should do. Rather, the CP and the maxims, with the assistance of implicatures, help explain how utterances are understood. Consider the following exchange.

Example 4.1

Police officer: Can you step out of the car?
Driver: Yes [but driver does not move].

Even if the speaker were not a police officer, everyone would understand this question as a request to get out of the car. It is clearly a speech act, a request or order. It is not an imperative, but asking whether someone 'can' do something is a conventional way of asking them to do it; it is an indirect speech act (Searle, 1975). However, the driver in this instance has chosen to interpret the officer's words literally, as a request for information.

- There is a difference between the (literal) meaning of an utterance and its message.
- Grice's Co-operative Principle and maxims help explain how people arrive at the message.

Not wanting to say

Before moving on to some examples, it is helpful to explain some of the terminology associated with the CP. First, I deal with ways in which a maxim can be unfulfilled, as there is more than one way in which this can be done. Probably the most important kind of non-fulfilment is the flout. As shown, flouting leads to implicature.

Sometimes people cannot fulfil a maxim because of other circumstances. For example, once a promise has been made not to divulge some information, there will be questions that cannot be answered (Grice, 1989, pp. 30–1). There are some choices about how to manage questions asking for the secret information. One is to explicitly 'opt out'; this involves telling the questioner that a promise to keep a secret has been made. The speaker may also be faced with a 'clash'. This occurs when fulfilling one maxim would lead to the violation of another. If a person is being questioned about her whereabouts on a particular day at a particular time and this pertains to the secret, a 'clash' will arise between the maxims of quality and quantity. Finally, it is also possible to deny any knowledge of the secret information (without mentioning the secret). This will 'violate' a maxim (in this case, the maxim of quality). The violation is an interesting case, particularly in a legal context. Grice describes it in the following way:

> He [sic] may quietly and unostentatiously *violate* a maxim; if so, in some cases he will be liable to mislead (1989, p. 30).

The adverbs are significant here; 'quietly' and 'unostentatiously'. If a speaker violates the maxim of quality in this way, it is very difficult – if not impossible – to know that a violation has occurred. This is important for a few reasons. First, if there is no sign that a violation has taken place there cannot be any implicature (this is the difference between a violation and a flout). Second, if the violation really is quiet and unostentatious there will be no sign of it in the utterance itself. Note that this does not rule out the possibility that other facts, information or knowledge may expose the violation; but this other information is extraneous to the speech context and the utterance itself.

Even if other information is available that brings the violation to light, the only implicature-type result possible will be what can be called a 'social implicature' (Greenall, 2009) or 'social implication' (Mooney, 2004). Discovering that a violation occurred will suggest something about the speaker; that she is untrustworthy for example. But, there can be no implicature which indicates, for example, what the truth really is. Theories may be generated from other information, from social implications and so on, but there will be nothing in the language itself which can be used.

Presupposition

Like violations, presuppositions are also hidden, but they can be found, as they are 'hidden' in plain sight. They are found exactly, and only, by paying attention to what is said. The concept and working of presupposition is very straightforward, but it has been made slightly more difficult because of the way 'implicature' is sometimes used as a synonym for 'presupposition'. The most commonly used example of presupposition actually comes from a legal frame.

Activity 4.3

Mr Smith has never beaten his wife. Exactly how should he answer the following?

Lawyer: Mr Smith, tell me, when did you stop beating your wife?

If Mr Smith has never so much as raised a finger against his wife, answering this question is going to take some time. This is because of the presupposition that Mr Smith has, at some point, beaten his wife. The operation of presupposition in this way can be very effective, and is often described as the 'premise' of the question. It is also possible to see presuppositions as treating something which is new as given.

There is a straightforward way to test for presuppositions, as they remain present even if the sentence is negated. Consider:

Example 4.2

Mr Smith, tell me, when did you not stop beating your wife.

Note that the question also presupposes that Mr Smith has a wife. It would make no sense to say:

Example 4.3

Mr Smith has stopped beating his wife and/but Mr Smith doesn't have a wife.

This demonstrates that presuppositions are not always interesting or controversial. The important point about presuppositions is that they are embedded in the utterance; the utterance treats the presuppositions as absolutely unproblematic.

Presupposition is sometimes labelled 'semantic presupposition', in contrast to 'pragmatic presupposition'. Whereas a semantic presupposition is embedded in the sentence, a pragmatic presupposition is best described as an inference or implicature, something that the speaker can assume the hearer will know or understand. Remember that an implicature has to be generated by the hearer to make 'sense' of the utterance. By contrast, an inference is a conclusion the hearer may reasonably come to; but it is not logically entailed by an utterance, nor is it the result of implicature. Thus, an inference generally involves applying some kind of common sense, or shared knowledge, to an interaction.

Grice's maxims are often found in normal conversation. In a legal setting, they can take on particular significance, as the rules that apply in a legal context do not always match up with the rules for 'normal' conversation. The maxims can still be used; they just need to be framed in terms of the specific activity taking place (Attardo, 1993; Levinson, 1992).

- Non-fulfilment of maxims can happen in a number of ways.
- This may lead to implicature or social implicature.
- The violation can be particularly difficult to detect.
- Presuppositions are embedded in an utterance.
- Presuppositions remain true even if the utterance is negated.

A meeting with the law

As Chapter 3 showed, the conventions around speech acts are modified when police are present (especially if they are armed). Some short examples will show how this works in relation to the maxims. What is interesting in these examples is that while implicatures of the conventional kind are present, they also generate social implications.

Example 4.4

1. Police 1: You got a gun in the car?
2. Man: It's my wife's. She left it in the car.
3. Police 1: Come on. Let's go back over here to the car.
4. Man: It's in my pocket. I'm going to take it to my wife.
5. Police 2: It's in your pocket now?
6. Man: Yes Sir.

Example 4.5

[later in the same interaction]
7. Man: It's not mine sir. I'm telling you.
8. Police 1: I don't care whose it is. It was in your pocket. Concealed. Loaded.
9. Man: But there was no bullet in the trigger or whatever you call it.
10. Police 2: Doesn't matter.
11. Man: See. I didn't know that. I've never. I'm a bounty hunter, I did not know this kind of stuff.

12. Police 2: How do you not have a permit to carry a gun when you're a bounty
    hunter?

(Examples and analysis from Linfoot-Ham, 2006, pp. 32–3)

Activity 4.4

Which maxims are relevant in this encounter? What will the police think
of this man? Is implicature involved?

In Example 4.4, there is flouting of the maxim of quantity in the first
two lines. Instead of the man simply answering 'Yes' to the police officer's question, he explains that the gun is his wife's. (Note the presupposition that he has a wife.) This answer leads conventionally (by
implicature) to an affirmation of the officer's question. However, in the
context of the interaction, a better response may have been simply
'yes'. In lay terms, there is an expectation that people 'co-operate' with
the police. In Gricean terms, this means that responses should probably not require the police to generate an implicature.

In Example 4.5, it is possible to argue that the man is flouting the
maxims of quantity and relevance. It is clear from the officer's words in
line 8, 'I don't care' that there is very little the man can say. While the
officer's 'I don't care' seems to flout the maxim of relevance, it may
indicate that the police officer has already decided that the man is
flouting the maxim of relevance and quantity. In short, the suspect has
said enough. It is not so much that the officer personally does not care,
but rather that the law is indifferent to anything more. In fact, the
man's continued talking (flouting the maxim of quantity) gets him into
more trouble. Revealing that he is a bounty hunter makes the police
officer even more suspicious. Drawing on his knowledge of bounty
hunters, the police officer questions the claim made by the man in line
11. For the officer, this statement suggests that the man is violating the
maxim of quality (Linfoot-Ham, 2006, p. 33); if the man really is a
bounty hunter he would probably know about gun laws and he would
have his own gun. Note that detecting the violation relies on knowledge drawn from outside the interaction itself.

By examining data, riding along with police officers and interviewing them, Linfoot-Ham argues that, for police officers, the maxim of

quality is probably the most important (2006, p.38). It is also the most difficult to judge. She argues that politeness is also very important (2006, p. 35), and while this is not a Gricean maxim, his framework does not rule it out. However, in conversations with the police, non-fulfilment of the maxims of manner, relevance and quantity can all lead to suspicion of a violation (2006, p. 38). The implicature that results is a social implication/social implicature, specifically, that there is a violation of the maxim of quality.

Even having seen what can happen in a police interaction, when dealing with implicature, presuppositions and the like, it is important to remember that none of these are suspicious or deceptive of them-selves. These are exploited in ordinary conversation simply because it is an efficient (and indeed conventional) way of getting a message across.

Activity 4.5

Look at the extract below. What kind of person is the interviewee? Is he a witness, a suspect or an expert of some kind? Point to as much evidence in the transcript as possible.

1. Police interviewer: There's certain facts I need to make you aware of at this stage. I don't think there can be any dispute in a lot of them. Mrs Mellor's body was buried on the 18th May 1998 at Highfield Cemetery, Stockport. Would you accept that from me?
2. Interviewee: If you say.
3. Police interviewer: Now would you also accept that the body of Mrs Mellor was exhumed with consent of the Coroner on the 22nd of September this year?
4. Interviewee: If you say so.
5. Police interviewer: And I think, from what you were saying earlier, you were aware that a post-mortem examination was subsequently undertaken. Certain samples were taken at that post-mortem for forensic analysis. Would you accept that?
6. Interviewee: You're telling the story, yes of course.
7. Police interviewer: A Home Office pathologist – Dr Rutherford – carried out that post-mortem examination. I think as you were going to mention, his findings do not support that this lady died of a coronary thrombosis as you diagnosed. Would you like to make any comment on that – that finding?
8. Interviewee: Doctors don't always diagnose a heart attack as a heart attack, they'll call it a coronary thrombosis or myocardial ischaemia

or myocardial infarction. To the average run of the mill GP they are all the same – the patient's dead. With a coronary thrombosis you'd expect that there'd be a bit of heart that's sort of damaged but you can have had just an electrical disorganisation of the heart which kills you just as effectively and leaves no symptoms at all – no signs, sorry, signs at all.

9. Police interviewer: Well in his expert opinion there was nothing to support your diagnosis is what I'm saying.

10. Interviewee: And he couldn't rule out a disorganised electrical activity in the heart.

11. Police interviewer: Forensic examination of the samples taken, including muscle tissue, at that post-mortem have been examined. These are the samples taken from Mrs Mellor. And there's certainly a high level of morphine still contained in her body – a fatal level to be precise. Can you account for that?

12. Interviewee: No.

(Newbury and Johnson, 2006, p. 233; see also BBC News, 2000)

This is part of the data Newbury and Johnson (2006) use to examine resistance of police questioning routines (see also Haworth, 2006). The questions and answers here are odd for a few reasons. The first is that the interviewer asks questions that do not serve the purpose questions normally do. Usually, a question is a way of getting information. However, questions (1), (3) and (5) *provide* information; they are 'confirmation seeking' questions. The interviewee might be expected to answer 'yes' to all of these. But the form of his answers 'If you say' and 'You're telling the story' suggest that he does not treat them as 'proper' questions.

The question in (7) is also a strange kind of question. It could be analysed as a flout of the maxim of manner as it is not very clear what the question is asking. Thus, the message might be put as follows: 'Do you still maintain that the woman died of a coronary thrombosis' or, more succinctly, 'You lied didn't you?'. This interview can also be understood as a performance for another audience, as it will form part of the evidence used in a criminal trial. Thus, in (11) the police officer asks the interviewee whether he can 'explain' the presence of morphine in the body. The interviewee responds with a simple 'No'. The question answer pair here has been constructed to imply, to allow a later audience to infer, that the interviewee is guilty.

The nature of the questions and the facts covered suggest that the interviewee is a suspect. This is an extract from police interviews with Harold Shipman, a GP found guilty of causing the death of a number of elderly patients under his care (see Shipman Archive, 2005). Once this is known, it is very difficult to see his responses as anything but evasive, clever and deceptive. But consider this: if he was in fact innocent, how might he have answered these questions differently? An innocent interviewee might be very likely to answer the questions in the same way that Shipman did. I am not suggesting anything about the particular case of Harold Shipman. The point is, in some situations there just is not a 'good' answer to a question.

- The Co-operative Principle and presupposition can work differently in a legal context.
- They work differently because of the rules and conventions of speaking and interpretation which apply in many legal situations.
- Legal conversations may be designed with another audience in mind.

Is silence golden?

If a suspect is innocent, it might be best not to say anything at all. As silence is the opposite of speech it is tempting to think that it communicates nothing at all. However, a distinction can be made between silence that does not communicate anything and that which does (Kurzon, 2007). The latter is 'communicative silence' (Sobkowiak, 1997, p. 44) and a couple of examples will make the distinction clear.

Activity 4.6

What is the meaning of silence in each of the following?

Example 4.6

Lawyer: Were you at the garage on the evening of the 26th of May 2012?
Witness: [no response].

Example 4.7

Sally: What time did you say we should be at the party?
George: [no response].

These two examples show that context is significant in the interpretation of silence. In Example 4.6, the names of the participants indicate that this exchange is taking place in a formal setting. It may be a courtroom or during the taking of an official statement or affidavit. If Grice's maxims are applied, it is not clear what the witness is doing. The silent response suggests a violation, but in this context, it is not really 'unostentatious'. Further, as Grice defines a flout such that it does not include the clash, it seems more likely that the witness is faced with a clash; to fulfil the maxim of quantity would mean violating the maxim of quality. Given that witnesses are sworn to obey the maxim of quality, this would be a reasonable conclusion. Nevertheless, it is not clear what the implicature would be. Perhaps all that can be said is that the witness has something to hide. This would be an inference, or a social implicature. One might argue that the 'obvious' meaning of silence in Example 4.6 is that the witness has something to hide. But this is only obvious if there is a conversational convention that tells us this is the right way to interpret the silence. Such a convention would make the silence 'communicative' (but see Chapter 6).

Example 4.7 is not so clear cut; this is because of the setting in which the exchange takes place. There are a number of reasons George may not have answered. Many of these are social implications; George may be annoyed with Sally and be giving her 'the silent treatment', he may not have heard the question and so on. In this context, there is no single convention that would tell us what George's silence means. Sally may generate some hypotheses and then test them; for example, she may first try repeating the question more loudly. In short, it is not clear whether George's silence is communicative at all.

What silence means in a legal context is often stipulated by the law itself. This is clear when the rights of detailed people in different countries are considered (see Gibbons, 2001; Rock, 2007). Up until 1994 in the UK, someone being arrested would be told (Cotterill, 2000, p. 6):

You do not have to say anything unless you wish to do so, but what you say may be given in evidence.

A change in the law (The Criminal Justice and Public Order Act, 1994, sections 34–8) resulted in a change to the caution (Cotterill, 2000, p. 6):

> You do not have to say anything, but it may harm your defence if you do not mention when questioned something which you later rely on in court. Anything you do say may be given in evidence.

Activity 4.7

What is the difference between these two formulations? Does a detained person in the UK have a right to silence?

Whether people in the UK have a right to silence will depend on what 'right' means, as well as on how the first clause of the caution is understood. The caution begins by explicitly telling the detainee that she does 'not have to say anything'. However, the following 'but …' clause qualifies this; and as Cotterill notes, it also doubles the length of the caution (2000, p. 6). It is probably not entirely clear to the addressee of this warning what this 'but' clause is doing as it has a complex construction with a great deal of subordination; '*but* it may harm your defence *if* you do not mention *when* questioned something *which* you later rely on in court' (my emphasis).

The legislation that brought about the change provides some insight, as it stipulates that silence ('failure to mention') can be used by the court to 'draw such inferences from the failure as appear proper' (Criminal Justice and Public Order Act 1994, s. 34). This appears to mean that 'ordinary' conversational rules can be applied to silences, omissions or 'failures to mention' anything related to the case. This is problematic for at least two reasons. The first is that the person being questioned has already been told 'You do not have to say anything'. This looks like a right to silence. Second, talking to the police after being cautioned is hardly an 'ordinary conversation'. Even though the law stipulates how silence can be understood, it is not clear to whom the inferences have to 'appear proper', nor exactly what 'proper' means.

Remembering that conversations with the police are not 'ordinary' is also relevant for the meaning of 'mention' (Cotterill, 2000, pp. 17–18). To 'mention' something is to speak about it in a way that does not give it a great deal of emphasis. Moreover, the mentioning has to happen during questioning. As Cotterill makes clear, questioning by police generally involves the police asking questions to get information (2000, pp. 17–18). What if there is a crucial detail but the police do not ask a question about it? Is the suspect supposed to volunteer it? It has already been shown that it is not a good idea to flout the maxim of quantity or relevance when speaking with the police. If an appropriate question is not asked, it may be impossible in this interactional context to 'mention' crucial information.

Finally, the content of the 'but' clause needs to be considered.

> but it may harm your defence if you do not mention when questioned something which you later rely on in court.

This presupposes that the detainee has a defence, in the sense that she will have to defend herself in court. This presupposition has an entailment, that is, something that logically follows from it; there will be a trial. At this point, it is very difficult, if not impossible, for the detainee to know what kinds of information and evidence may be needed for this defence. In short 'The detained person is thus required to make an irrevocable evaluation, at the time of questioning, of which issues may become significant months later and in a totally different communicative context' (Cotterill, 2000, p. 20). Making this evaluation is hard enough, but knowing that this is the determination that needs to be made involves decoding a complex caution, one that it is difficult even for police officers to explain in their own words (Cotterill, 2000).

When a question is not a question

The situation in the US is not the same as in the UK, because US law stipulates that silence should be understood differently. The right to silence and a right against self-incrimination are both enshrined in the Fifth Amendment to the US Constitution. Detainees are advised of their right to silence with the Miranda warning. While American law does not stipulate a particular form of words for the Miranda warning (Shuy, 1997, p. 176), it generally looks something like this.

> You have the right to remain silent. Anything you say can and will be used against you in a court of law. You have the right to speak

to an attorney, and to have an attorney present during any questioning. If you cannot afford a lawyer, one will be provided for you at government expense (cited in Ephratt, 2008, p. 1929).

There are important differences between this and the UK caution. The Miranda warning specifically refers to 'the *right* to remain silent' and informs the detainee that anything that say *will* be used. The modal verb here is more emphatic and certain than the UK 'may'. The Miranda warning also points out the right to legal representation. This right is also part of UK law; it is just not part of the initial short caution (see Cotterill, 2000, p. 5). The Miranda warning, then, looks reasonably straightforward; 'You have the right to remain silent' is clear and emphatic. Nevertheless, there are still a number of unanswered questions about the Miranda warning, such as what does 'remain silent' mean and what has to be done to invoke the right to silence (Shuy, 1997).

It seems reasonable to think that the right to silence could be invoked simply by remaining silent. But what if the detainee asks for a glass of water or to use the bathroom? If the detainee says something, does this constitute a waiver of the right to silence? (Shuy, 1997, p. 189). It is also important to consider what a police officer might do when an arrestee remains silent. If the detainee does not speak, do the officers cease asking questions? Research demonstrates that they do not (Shuy, 1997); and if a detainee answers any questions, even after invoking their right to silence, their answers may still be admissible in court.

Janet Ainsworth (2008, 2010) has written extensively about the right to silence in the US. She has shown that American courts have decided that in order to invoke the right to silence, the detained person has to say something. Moreover, only some utterances 'count' as invoking the right to silence.

Activity 4.8

The following utterances have all been said by a person in the US who has been read their Miranda rights. What message is communicated in each instance? When considering these bear two things in mind: 1) the other rights that are included in the Miranda warning; 2) the conversational context, especially the power difference between police and detainee.

1. Could I get my lawyer?
2. Actually, you know what, I'm gonna call my lawyer. I don't feel comfortable.
3. I think I would like to talk to a lawyer.
4. I don't have anything to say.
5. I don't wanna talk no more.
6. I don't feel like I can talk with you without an attorney sitting right here to give me some legal advice.
7. I'll be honest with you. I'm scared to say anything without talking to a lawyer.

(All from Ainsworth, 2008)

The courts held that none of these were enough to invoke the right to silence. Ainsworth reports that the first did not count as it was interpreted as a question. Numbers 2 and 3 were construed as mitigated and hence not requests. 4 and 5 were too 'ambiguous or equivocal' (Ainsworth, 2008, p. 9) and 6 and 7 were construed as requests for a lawyer.

A detainee needs to use a direct, un-hedged request for legal assistance, for example, 'Give me a lawyer', or state declaratively that she is invoking her right to silence, for example, 'I am exercising my Constitutional right to silence'. This may seem reasonable until the context and the rules of conversation are considered. As discussed above, politeness is very important when dealing with the police. Indirect requests are a common way of being polite. As Ainsworth points out, in normal conversations questions and indirect requests routinely function as requests (2008, p. 11). Moreover, according to normal conversational rules, a request for a lawyer should probably count as invoking the right to silence, as the right to silence and to legal representation are both included in the Miranda warning. This situation shows the difference between ordinary rules of conversational interaction and the rules that apply in legal settings. The difference, however, is not apparent on the face of the interaction; the detainee has no way of knowing that a different set of rules apply in this particular case.

Ainsworth argues that the law approaches language in a particular way. Drawing on her work as a linguist and lawyer, and on her work about invoking the right to silence in the USA, she sets out the ideas that seem to underpin legal understandings of language and communication.

1. Language is a medium that maps human thought on to an objective external reality and it does so transparently.
2. A person's own mental states – such as desire or intent – are part of externally verifiable objective reality.
3. Language is best understood objectively, from the point of view of what a reasonable person would think something meant, not subjectively from the point of view of idiosyncratic speakers and hearers. Therefore, language is best understood by reference to authoritative sources on objective meaning.
4. People have an obligation to use language transparently and bear the responsibility if they fail to use language precisely and appropriately.
5. Therefore, it is fair to hold people to the objective meaning entailed by the language that they use, irrespective of what they subjectively intended that language to mean (Ainsworth, 2008, pp. 14–16).

These ideas suggest that communication is very straightforward. Moreover, the control people are required to have over the production and reception of language is something like the control they are expected to have over their physical bodies. If a person hits someone, she is held to be accountable for this. But language is different because utterances can be construed according to different rules over which there is little or no control. In a legal context, the particular interpretative regimes in operation can be particularly opaque.

- Maxims operate in police and legal encounters according to the conventions of those contexts.
- These conventions and rules operate even though they may be hidden.

Conclusion

The Co-operative Principle and the four maxims can be very useful in explaining how communication takes place. In particular settings, like dealing with police officers, they may need to be framed by a second set of rules in order to explain the interaction. This embedding of Grice in another context is not unique to the legal setting, but it makes clear that while legal conversations sometimes function according to the normal rules, there may also be important differences. The fact that different rules apply is not itself problematic. The problem arises when these rules are not made clear but people are, nevertheless, held accountable to them. If these rules of interpretation are provided, it is important that they are clear and easily understood.

5

The trials of language

This chapter looks at questions, paying attention to the effects they can have in an interaction. I begin by looking at how witness statements are taken and constructed as questions are central to this process. These are important texts, which may form the basis of a criminal trial. Attention then turns to the way lawyers question witnesses and suspects in the courtroom. The effect of particular questions in the courtroom depends on the structure of the trial and the communicative rules of this context. Therefore, some detail about the stages of a criminal trial will be given.

Stating and statements

Written texts are very important in the law (Tiersma, 2001a). In a criminal trial, witness statements, as well as those taken from suspects, are significant pieces of evidence. During a trial, lawyers may ask witnesses about the details contained in their statements; either to introduce this information into court or to challenge its veracity. If what a witness says at trial differs too much from what is in the statement, the witness may appear to be unreliable (Komter, 2002).

Many jurisdictions stipulate that the witness statement should be in the witnesses' own words (Komter, 2006, p. 206; Rock, 2001, p. 44). However, a very common way of taking statements is through question and answer. In the following, bold indicates typing by the police officer (P). S is the suspect and 'Fame' is a store which figures in the account being given by the suspect.

Example 5.1

13. P: (types, 5 seconds:)
14. **Fame was before that.**
15. P: Why don't you first tell me about Fame then
16. What what uh happened there
17. Fame is in the Kalverstraat, right?
18. S: Yes.
19. P: Quite near Dam Square right?
20. S: Yes.
21. P: (types, 16 seconds:)
22. **Fame is in the Kalverstraat in Amsterdam, quite near Dam Square.**

(Komter, 2006, p. 206)

The facts here might not appear to be very interesting; the location of the store may seem either entirely irrelevant or completely obvious. Nevertheless, all the details, and words, that end up in typed lines are provided by the police officer. As he has access to information about the incident, this is not about the officer fabricating a statement, or making up facts. But the question remains: is it possible to say that the statement is in the words of the suspect?

When events and actions are described, the importance of police questioning becomes clearer. Like Komter, Rock (2001) pays close attention to the development of a witness statement. She traces the 'genesis' of the statement through various stages of questioning. The relevant incident in the case considered here involved alcohol, arguing and eventually a death. Specific moments are revisited time and again in the police questioning of witnesses; there at least four versions of the event (Rock, 2001, p. 52). While the witness begins in version one by telling the story, in version two the police officer asks questions about details in that narrative. In version three, details which have been adduced are checked, before the statement is taken down in version four.

Compare the versions of the same event given here. I is the interviewing officer and W is the witness. The numbers in parenthesis indicate a period of silence; (.) is a short pause, numbers indicate duration of the silence in seconds.

Example 5.2

Version 3

I: was he still in the chair at this time?
W: (.) yeh.
I: yeh, (.) and you say he was proper drunk?
W: yeh.
I: (.) OK (.) y-you said some was it how long (.) before the man flipped?
W: say about phhh (.) not quite sure because they was quite – arguing for quite a long time.
I: (10.2) OK and suddenly the man flips?

Example 5.3

Version 4

I: OK (10.4) so when you say he wa – he continued to argue a bit, is that when he was shouting (.) urm (.) you bastards I'll knock you out?
W: yeh.
I: (9.2) who was he saying that to?
W: to Kegs.
I: (11.8) he said that to Kevin (2.9) this went on for how long?
W: about not actsh – not actually sure how long it went (.) on for.
I: how long do you think?
W: say about (.) say about 10 minutes.
I: (4.2) this went on for about 10 minutes (.) suddenly the man flip – flipped.

The relevant part of the final statement reads:

> I said don't start arguing in the man's house and they calmed down, the man continued to argue a bit saying 'you bastards I'll knock you out' he was saying that to Kevin [surname]
>
>   This went on for 10 minutes. Suddenly the man flipped (Rock, 2001, pp. 64–5).

Activity 5.1

How many of the witness's words are in the final statement? Is it enough to count the words?

While some of the words used by the witness do make it into the final statement, the clauses do not. For example, the witness seemed unsure about the timing of the argument, eventually offering 'say about 10 minutes'. But it is included in the statement in a rather less hedged manner. What began as a witness's rough estimation has been turned into a fact; it is a fact which can now be used to challenge the witness in court (Rock, 2001, p. 65). Komter observes, 'The interrogator collapses his questions and the suspect's confirmations into a written text that can later be attributed to the suspect' (2006, p. 206).

Pointing out the difference between what the witness said and what is recorded in the statement is not about criticising what the police officers are doing. Both Komter and Rock make clear that the statement serves a number of purposes and, thus, the officer constructing it has to make sure that it is fit for all of those uses. A police officer putting a statement together is constantly shifting footing, taking on different roles. She orients to the person in front of her, to the task of putting together a detailed and coherent narrative which complies with the rules of the statement genre, and also thinks ahead to the legal construction and understanding of the statement in an investigation and trial. All of these objectives are fused together in the final statement. (There is a similar kind of 'working' of witness statements in civil cases (Tyrwhitt-Drake, 2003).) Research like Komter's and Rock's shows what actually happens during statement taking and makes it possible to work back from a real statement to reasonable hypotheses about what actually happened during the interaction (see Chapter 8).

Some of these hypotheses are easier to generate than others. Portions of the statement included for very specific legal reasons can look very strange until the routines followed in statement taking and construction are considered. Interactions like the following often occur towards the end of statement taking sessions with suspects.

Example 5.4

1. P: Do you realize that it is forbidden in the Netherlands to uh have cocaine on you,
2. or to deal in it?
3. S: (nods)
4. P: (types, 24 seconds:) I know that it is forbidden in the Netherlands to possess cocaine or to deal in it.

(Komter, 2003, p. 205)

Example 5.6

P: Did Melvin give you permission to throw the hammer at his front door?
(pause)
S: NO!!

(Stokoe and Edwards, 2008, p. 91)

These have been called 'silly questions' (Stokoe and Edwards, 2008) and on the face of it, given the information available to the conversational participants, they are rather redundant. At the same time, given the importance of written texts in the law, it is important that these details are included. These questions often enumerate the separate elements of an offence. There may be similar questions asked of the victim. For example, Melvin will be asked whether he gave permission for a hammer to be thrown at his front door. These questions ensure that the suspect's '"intentions and knowledge", or "state of mind" with regard to the actions they have already admitted carrying out, are made explicit "for the record"' (Stokoe and Edwards, 2008, p. 107).

• Witness statements are highly constructed texts.
• The statements are not always in the words of the witness.
• The texts are subsequently treated as reliable.

The courtroom context

Once all the materials necessary for the trying of a criminal case have been assembled, and a decision has been made to prosecute, the trial can commence. In this section, I look at interaction in the courtroom itself, concentrating on the questions that lawyers ask witnesses and the accused. As the examples used are from a British criminal case involving a jury and barristers, I follow that terminology here when discussing the specific interactions. Different jurisdictions have different rules regarding who can represent clients in courts and, of course, not all trials involve a jury.

Activity 5.2

Drawing on any knowledge you may have, make a note of all the participants you can think of in a courtroom. Think about what these people do. This should help you to come up with some initial ideas about what kinds of speaking rules apply in the courtroom.

A list of participants should include judges, lawyers, witnesses and the jury. There are a number of other people in a courtroom – clerks to the court, stenographers and ushers – but, like jurors, they have very limited speaking rights when it comes to the observable business of the court. Even the lawyers and witnesses are subject to rules about the kinds of things they can say and when they can say them. The best way of seeing what this looks like is to go to a local court and observe for a couple of hours.

Being familiar with the structure of a trial helps to understand the interactional rules. In countries where British legal traditions have been adopted ('common law' systems, e.g., USA, Australia, Canada), an 'adversarial' system is used for trials. Each side has an advocate to present their case, then a third party assesses each argument and decides which is more persuasive. The third party will be a judge or a jury depending on the kind of case it is. Of course, there are standards that this third party needs to apply; they have to pay attention to the evidence, for example. Another important feature of this system is that the defendant is innocent until proven guilty. In contrast, 'civil law' systems (e.g., France, Germany and Japan) tend to adopt an inquisitorial approach. Here, the third party – usually a judge – conducts her own investigation. She interviews witnesses, takes statements and works directly with the police. The defendant needs to demonstrate her innocence.

In an adversarial trial, each side prepares and presents a case. In a criminal trial, opening statements are made by each side, and then the case for the prosecution is presented in its entirety, including all the witnesses they may wish to call. After this, the defence presents its argument. When each witness is called, there is an examination-in-chief (UK)/direct examination (USA), followed by a cross-examination. The side calling the witness conducts the examination-in-chief, and the opposing side then conducts the cross-examination. In jury trials, the judge will speak after the presentation of both sides. She will instruct the jury about the law they need to apply (Chapter 9) and, in the UK, she summarises the evidence presented and the arguments made in the trial.

Probably the most important rule in the courtroom situation is that the lawyers ask questions and the witnesses answer them. Here, I draw on some of the terminology and techniques of Conversation Analysis (CA) (Sacks, Schegloff and Jefferson, 1974). CA looks at the detail of conversations paying attention to what is said, pauses, intonation and the smallest details of talk. CA refers to the utterance of words by a speaker as a 'turn' and the alternation of speakers as 'turn taking'. In CA, the question/answer sequence is a particular kind of turn taking and is called an 'adjacency pair'; a question is followed by an answer, hence they are adjacent. It is possible to be more specific than this in relation to questions as there are different kinds. 'Open' questions allow the addressee a deal of latitude in their answer. These tend to begin with 'who', 'what', 'where' and 'why'. 'Closed' questions, on the other hand, invite a limited range of responses. 'Do you understand?' asks for a 'yes' or 'no' response. Moreover, with closed questions there is often a 'preferred' and a 'dispreferred' response. The question 'You're coming right?' has a preferred response, 'yes' and a dispreferred response 'no'. It is 'easier' to give the preferred response and the form of the question will usually indicate what the preferred response is. It can take more work to give a dispreferred response, and a pause may precede such an answer. Because they limit responses, and because they may suggest an answer is more welcome than another, closed questions can be very useful in the courtroom. They are useful not only in eliciting information, but also in controlling the way this information is presented. It makes sense, then, to say that closed questions generally exert more control over a witness than open questions.

Activity 5.3

Consider the following questions. How controlling would you say they were? Why? Does it depend on who is asking?

1. What happened on that evening?
2. Where were you standing then?
3. Were you angry or were you furious?
4. That's not what happened is it?
5. You were not happy about the situation. Is that not the case?
6. You weren't there.

As well as questions being open or closed, they can also be described as either 'information seeking' or 'confirmation seeking' (Newbury and Johnson, 2006, p. 218). The former tend to be open (as in 1 and 2) and the latter tend to be closed (as in 4 and 5). Both kinds of questions can be more or less constraining, in other words, coercive. For confirmation seeking questions, examples with tags like (4) are less constraining than bare declaratives, like example (6). While some information seeking questions will be very open like example (1), others are not. In example (3) the witness is very constrained, invited to choose between only two options. Of course, the witness can dispute the terms of the question but there are two things to notice: first, not responding directly to the terms of the question may be seen as being uncooperative; second, in offering only those two alternatives ('angry' and 'furious') the lawyer has set a semantic minefield. The witness will probably have to explicitly deny being 'angry' or 'furious' and thus the words will have been uttered again (Cotterill, 2004; see Chapter 9).

Questioning strategies during examination-in-chief and cross-examination are not as straightforward as one might imagine (Luchjenbroers, 1997; Woodbury, 1984). It is not the case that the former only uses open and the latter only closed questions. While it is possible to look at individual questions, and describe them in terms of being information or confirmation seeking, or in terms of control and coercion, each question and answer pair is part of a broader structure. As the examples that follow show, both the prosecution and the defence in a criminal trial make use of a range of questions. For example, if the preceding questions establish a particular set of facts, an open question can be particularly effective in a cross-examination.

- Questions can be open or closed.
- Questions may have a preferred answer.
- Questions may be confirmation seeking or information seeking.

Examining examination

In the previous chapter, transcripts of police interviews with Harold Shipman were examined. Here, attention is paid to the way the lawyers questioned him in the courtroom. The following testimony concerns Dr Shipman's interactions with Mrs Grundy, whom he was found guilty of murdering. A lengthy extract has been used here as it shows how individual questions function, as well as illustrating that lawyers use a variety of question types (McPeake, 2010, p. 156). Understanding how questioning works in the courtroom requires that attention be given not just to individual adjacency pairs, but also to the 'line' of questioning.

Activity 5.4

Look at the following examination-in-chief for open and closed questions. Is there a line of questioning or is the order of questions not important?

1. Q. Right. That was dealing with the wax in her ears. Was there any other conversation between the two of you?
   A. Yes.
2. Q. What took place?
   A. She produced some paper or papers out of her bag and asked if I would be kind enough to witness her signature.
3. Q. And when you say she produced a paper or papers, can you recall now what size the paper or papers were?
   A. The papers were folded so I would have thought A3 size.
4. Q. And she asked if you would?
   A. Witness her signature.
5. Q. And what did you say?
   A. I jokingly said to her that if it was a will and she was going to leave me some money I couldn't do it.
6. Q. And what was her response to that?
   A. There was a moment's pause and I realised that it was something like that and I said I would get a couple of patients to come and do it.

7. MR. JUSTICE FORBES: Sorry, I didn't quite catch the last part of that, 'There was a moment's pause. I realised it was something like that?'
   A. And I said I would get two people out of the waiting room.

8. MR. JUSTICE FORBES: Thank you.
   [lines omitted]

9. Q. When Mrs. Grundy either produced the document, put it on the table, left it on the table, was there ever a time when you touched any sheet of paper produced by Mrs. Grundy on the 9th June?
   A. Yes.

10. Q. When?
    A. When Mrs. Grundy took the document or documents, and I really can't remember if there was more than one piece of paper, as she asked me and I was refusing I pushed the paper back to her. So I sort of pushed my finger across like that and gave it back to her.

11. Q. And the part that you were pushing back, was that a part on which there was any writing? If you cannot remember please don't speculate?
    A. I can't remember.

12. Q. You have told us that on that occasion you placed was it one or more fingers on the document, Dr. Shipman?
    A. At least one.

13. Q. Was that the only occasion upon which you touched a document produced by Mrs. Grundy on the 9th June?
    A. No.

14. Q. What other occasion or occasions did you touch any such document produced?
    A. After the two witnesses had signed I picked up the paper or more than one piece of paper and handed it back to Mrs. Grundy.

(Shipman Archive, 2005)

These lines deal with the alleged signing and witnessing of a will. Notice that the barrister moves between open and closed information seeking questions. Question 2 is very open, while question 3 is quite specific, relating to the size of the papers. The first few questions and answers seem to be designed to let Shipman tell a story; open questions are used. Thus, he is able to report that he 'jokingly' said that if he was being left money he could not witness Mrs Grundy's signature (5). He further recounts that a pause from Mrs Grundy confirmed his thought. At this point, the relevance of these events is not clear. The second part of the extract is rather more specific, dwelling on the handling of paper. Notice that the barrister is quite careful to ask questions about 'paper or more than one piece of paper' here. This, along with other features of the examination-in-chief, anticipates material to be covered in the cross-examination. Barristers are instructed to 'insulate [their] witness from attack by [the] opposition in cross-examination. That may mean getting the witness to talk about topics relevant to your opponent's case' (McPeake, 2010, p. 138).

Given the nature of the examination-in-chief, one might expect to find only open questions; looking at real examples demonstrates that this is not the case. Closed questions need to be used because evidence has to be introduced into court and because of the rules of speaking in the court the only way this can be done is through a question and answer routine. Thus, at the start of the examination-in-chief, a great deal of time is spent going through a set of photographs and a floor plan of Dr Shipman's surgery. He is simply asked to identify what the photographs are. Of course, a more efficient way of doing this may be to provide a selection of images to the court with captions and then simply refer to them. But as the evidence has to be introduced into court, the question and answer structure is required.

The counter argument

Cross-examination is generally thought to be both more interesting and more dramatic than examination-in-chief. In the case of Shipman, note that it is the defence who conducted the examination-in-chief. The prosecution then follow with their cross-examination of the defence's witness.

1. Q. Mrs. Grundy was asking for your signature?
   A. She asked if I would sign the document.
2. Q. Isn't that the same thing?
   A. I am telling you that she asked me to sign the document.
3. Q. I said Mrs. Grundy was asking for your signature and I think you are agreeing with me?
   A. She was asking me to sign the document, she wasn't specifically asking me for a signature which she could take away.
4. Q. I see. So your response to that was, 'No, I will get two patients.' Why two patients and not one?
   A. Because she had asked.

5. Q. No?

A. She had asked me to sign it and I had surmised that it was a will and therefore I knew you need two signatures.

6. Q. You were very very quick on the uptake, weren't you, having just been asked for your signature, to decide quickly that you needed two people from the surgery, were you not?

A. I don't think I was particularly quick on the uptake. If it was a will and it needed witnessing—.

7. Q. Of course?

A. —it needed two signatures.

8. Q. Of course, if you were the person who prepared the document in the first place you would know that it was a will and you would know that you needed two people to sign a will, wouldn't you?

A. If I had done all what you have told me then I already would know that you need two signatures to witness a will.

9. Q. Now you say that Mrs. Hutchinson and Mr. Spencer signed the document that was there seen first by you in Mrs. Grundy's hand?

A. They signed a document which may well have been the document that I saw in Mrs. Grundy's hand.

10. Q. And your explanation for your little fingerprint being in the bottom left hand corner of this document is that you at some stage pushed the document across the desk and that explains your little finger on the face of the document?

A. That is probably the right conclusion to draw.

11. Q. It cannot conceivably be right, can it?

A. (No reply.).

12. Q. The document that you have there that bears your fingerprint was not the document signed by Mr. Spencer and Mrs. Hutchinson, was it?

A. I am told by the Court that that is so.

13. Q. And so your fingerprint could not have got on that piece of paper in the witness box with you now on that occasion, could it?

A. Yes.

14. Q. How?

A. I did say that she produced a document. I was not in the room all the time with her. And I don't know whether there was one piece of paper or two pieces of paper.

15. Q. Yes. I am going to have to ask you to look and see what you told the police. You are suggesting, are you, there may have been more than one piece of paper in Mrs. Grundy's possession there and then?

    A. I am saying I do not know if there was more than one piece of paper.

16. Q. I am sorry, you gave evidence about this matter earlier?

    A. I will accept then that I suggested there was more than one piece of paper in Mrs. Grundy's possession.

17. Q. You have already said Mrs. Grundy had more than one piece of paper in her possession when you gave evidence?

    A. Thank you for reminding me.

18. Q. I am going to remind you now of what you said to the police. Page 96 of the interview?

    A. Thank you. I have it.

19. Q. Thank you. Your reply, 'Mr. Spencer, and I asked if they would witness a signature and they came in and witnessed her signature. Mrs. Grundy had used my pen, something that I am not happy about people doing. I am sure if you have a favourite pen you know that you don't let other people use it, and I gave biros to the other two people and they witnessed her signature. They went out and I introduced, I said, 'This is Mrs. Grundy" They went out. We finished the consultation. She took the piece of paper that had been signed, put it in her bag and went out. I was not allowed to see what was written on the paper.' Does that answer the question? There you refer to the piece of paper, don't you?

    A. I actually used those words?

20. Q. Yes, and it was 'a piece of paper' was it not?

    A. At all times I don't know. (Shipman Archive, 2005)

Activity 5.5

Are the questions asked in the cross-examination the same as in the examination-in-chief? Does the content of the examination-in-chief make more sense now that the cross-examination can be seen?

The function of the cross-examination is to identify and then challenge inconsistencies in the witness's evidence. Here, the barrister challenges Shipman's previous testimony in its own terms and in relation to his interview with the police. The prosecution seeks to question the plausibility of the narrative that has already been given as well as to offer an alternative one, that is, that Shipman prepared the will and so knew exactly what the document was. The references to 'paper' or 'papers' in the direct examination now also make sense, as Shipman's fingerprint was found on a separate piece of paper.

In these questions, there are a few things that were not present in the lines taken from the examination-in-chief. The first is the marked use of commentary. This can be seen in question 6 when the barrister asks a question and, at the same time, comments on the witness and his evidence (Conley and O'Barr, 2005, p. 27–9). The tag, 'were you not' invites a 'yes' or 'no' answer (the 'preferred' being 'yes'), but Shipman provides something more elaborate. This may be precisely because the question is not so much a question as a commentary on the plausibility of Shipman's narrative. 'Such comments are not stated directly, but are embedded in questions' (Conley and O'Barr 2005, p. 27) as the question–answer routine has to be maintained. The use of commentary in this way also aligns with the 'two golden rules' of cross-examination:

1. Tell: don't ask! Include the answer you want in the question.
2. Lead, lead, lead – avoid open ended questions wherever and whenever possible. (McPeake, 2010, p. 167)

Things do not always run smoothly, though. Notice that it is possible to understand question 7 as an attempt by the barrister to cut Shipman off and continue to set out the alternative narrative. But Shipman resists, and appears to interrupt the barrister to finish the answer to question 6. While this is not a narrow transcription (we do not have indication of pauses, for example), such an interpretation does make sense of the 'Of course' in question 7, which seems to be an interrupted start to question 8 rather than being connected to anything the witness has said.

Question 11 provides an instance of something that is said to be typical of cross-examinations; silence (Conley and O'Barr, 2005, pp. 22–4). Moving back to the previous adjacency pair helps make sense of this. Question 10 asks Shipman to confirm what he has already said in the examination-in-chief, specifically, the explanation as to how his fingerprint came to be on a particular document. Question 11 is a direct challenge of his answer; but it is only a challenge. And while a question mark is indicated on the transcript, and 'no reply' is recorded there, is it really a question?

Activity 5.6

Is there any response that could have been given to 'question' 11? Think about what someone might say in a 'normal' conversation if challenged in this way.

What is the effect of the silence in this instance? What might the jury make of this? Who is responsible for the silence?

In a 'normal' conversation, question 11 might prompt the response 'why do you say that?' or 'what do you mean'? According to the rules of the courtroom, Shipman is not supposed to ask questions, he can only provide answers (even though he does ask a question in response to question 19). It is the barrister's task to ask questions; but the utterance at 11 is a question in name only. Using a rhetorical question in this context accomplishes a number of things. A rhetorical question does not 'expect' an answer; indeed, it often does not have an answer. Here, it serves to comment on the witness's testimony and to construct a silence. Only a lawyer can construct and exploit silence in this way (Conley and O'Barr, 2005, p. 23).

The last few lines of the cross-examination extract seek to contest exactly that which was raised in the examination-in-chief; whether there was only one piece of paper or whether there were more. The use of an open question in (14), where the barrister simply asks 'How?' is important. This asks how Shipman's fingerprint came to be on the piece of evidence. At this point, Shipman replies that he does not know how many pieces of paper there were. The barrister then asks a series of questions to confirm that this is what Shipman is saying; that he does not know how many pieces of paper. Once this has been firmly established, the barrister moves to the statement Shipman gave to the police where he specifically referred to 'a piece of paper'. It is clear that the jury are to understand this line of questioning as a demonstration of Shipman's dishonesty. Finally, the damning detail of the statement is immediately dropped as a topic. There is no way that Shipman can re-open the topic to provide another explanation. The rules of question and answer in the courtroom mean that only the barristers can indulge in this kind of 'topic management' (Conley and O'Barr, 2005, pp. 26–7). The open question at (14) is central to the point that the barrister has made: Shipman is lying.

These extracts show that understanding examination-in-chief and cross-examination needs more than just looking at individual questions. The examples demonstrate that an examination-in-chief uses open and closed questions and that it orients to the case that will be argued by the other side. A training manual for barristers puts the difference between examination-in-chief and cross-examination as follows:

> In general terms, examination-in-chief is about **trust**, the advocate allowing the witness the freedom to tell their story in their own words, but cross-examination is about **control**. The cross-examiner doesn't want the witness to tell their story in their own words; instead, the cross-examiner asks leading questions designed to convey the story of the cross-examiner's client in words chosen by the cross-examiner. (McPeake, 2010, p. 138; emphasis in original)

Nevertheless, control also has to be exercised during the examination-in-chief. But it is done 'more subtly, usually through selection of topics, [and] interventions when a witness strays into inadmissible or irrelevant information' (McPeake, 2010, p. 141). There is no doubt that because of their role in the trial and because of their professional training, lawyers in court are formidable users of language. What is important to note, however, is that their power derives from the linguistic and conversational rules that the court dictates – only barristers can ask questions and witnesses must respond – as well as from the conventions that apply to the conduct and understanding of any kind of conversation. Not responding to a question outside of the courtroom may also suggest that the individual has something to hide. Moreover, other more 'innocent' explanations – that the individual did not actually hear the question – are ruled out in the courtroom. Thus, while lawyers are experts at constructing questions and constructing narratives with these questions, they ultimately rely on the way questions are used in other situations.

- The courtroom has its own rules for speaking.
- Lawyers ask questions and witnesses answer them.

- There are strategies available to lawyers that are not available to witnesses.
- Different questions perform different functions; the questioning strategy can be seen in the choice and sequencing of questions.

Who is speaking to whom?

In discussing models of communication so far, attention has been given to the roles of speaker and hearer. But as Goffman (1981) points out, these positions can be further specified. In the case of the hearer, a hearer can be 'ratified' or 'un-ratified'. Both kinds of hearer have two further forms. A ratified hearer can either be 'addressed' or 'unaddressed'. In the case of the courtroom, a witness is ratified and addressed, but the jury, though ratified (in the sense of being a recognised presence in the court), are not directly addressed during the examination-in-chief and cross-examination. Un-ratified hearers include the inadvertent 'overhearer' and the engineered 'eavesdropper'. Un-ratified hearers generally occupy this role because of their own actions, rather than those of the speaker.

While it is possible to characterise the jury as ratified, non-addressed hearer, it is worth re-considering this. In a jury trial, these 12 men and women have an important role. They are tasked with assessing the evidence, establishing the facts and coming to a conclusion about the guilt or innocence of the accused. This means that courtroom interactions, such as the questioning of a witness, are best understood as addressed to the jury. Note that if the jury is the addressee, the addresser is not a person, but the interaction between lawyer and witness. Of course, lawyers want to control this interaction as much as possible, exactly because it constitutes an address to the jury.

When examining witnesses, lawyers can draw on a number of textual resources; records of interview and witness statements, for example (see Scheffer, 2007). When the barrister above quotes from Shipman's interview with police, he is speaking, but they are not his words. Again, Goffman provides a model that allows us to distinguish between the different texts and voices that are found in interactions (1981; see also Cotterill, 2004; and Heydon 2004). He distinguishes between the 'animator', 'author' and 'principal' (1981, p. 144). The animator gives voice to the text; she is 'the talking machine' (Goffman, 1981, p. 144). The author is the person who 'has selected the sentiments that are being expressed and the words in which they are encoded' (Goffman, 1981, p. 144), while the principal is the person 'whose position is established by the words that are spoken, someone whose beliefs have been told, someone who is committed to what the words say' (Goffman, 1981, p. 144).

In the context of Shipman's criminal trial, the principal in the cross-examination is the prosecution, the state. The principal is an institutional or rather abstract entity. The prosecution barrister ultimately speaks on behalf of the state, and, one might even say, on behalf of something like 'law and order' or 'justice'. The animator is composed of both the cross-examining barrister and Shipman in the example above; of course, in the cross-examination, the barrister will control the witness very carefully. The barrister and witness together comprise the author. In the cross-examination, the barrister will seek to be the author of as much as possible; in contrast, the examination-in-chief will allow the witness a larger slice of both the author and animator roles. As complex as this is, it is worth remembering that other people also contribute to the author role. In the UK, if a barrister is required, a solicitor will instruct her. The solicitor, then, will also play a role in the 'authoring' process.

Knowing precisely who occupies these roles for any specific question is not always obvious, at least not just from looking at the interaction. It may be, for example, that the police have developed a case theory which then informs the various questions that a lawyer asks. The lawyer has a representative role, but it is one that represents a number of other texts, positions, arguments and institutions. Bearing Goffman's framework in mind helps to remember that when lawyers speak in court, there may be a great deal of history behind their words.

- Courtroom interactions are highly structured.
- More than one person may contribute to the author, animator and principal roles.
- The question and answer routine can be understood as the addresser to an addressee; the jury.

Conclusion

To understand a text in the 'right' way, it may be necessary to have some insight into how it was produced. Without this, a text may be read in a way that does not represent the 'truth' even though the interpretation is valid with respect to the immediate evidence at hand. This is particularly important in relation to witnesses statements because these texts inform the questions asked in the courtroom. This chapter has also shown that being familiar with the rules of the courtroom is important in understanding how participants make their arguments. And while conversations in a legal context ultimately rely on the rules of 'normal' conversation, these everyday routines are also supplemented by and embedded in conventions stipulated by the law, its practices and institutions.

6

Different language different rules

Even in the most mundane situations, knowing which legal obligations apply can be difficult. In the context of an encounter with law enforcement, what is at stake can be very important. The witness interview and the language of the courtroom (Chapter 5) have shown that communicating what one wishes to say is not always straightforward. This may be related to the parallel linguistic world of the law and the ideology of language that seems to operate in the legal context (Chapter 4). At the heart of this is the belief that communication is, in one sense at least, absolutely straightforward. The idea that language is objective and that meaning can be ascertained is an important belief for the law to hold on to because otherwise decision making would be even more difficult. But as both linguists and lawyers know, things are not straightforward. This is especially true when a number of languages are present in a legal context.

Not the standard variety

The variety of language a person uses in the courtroom may have an effect on how they are perceived. For example, it has been suggested that witnesses may seem less credible if using non-Standard English. But to talk about non-standard English assumes that there is such a thing as Standard English and that it is widely and routinely used by English speakers (Trudgill, 2011). This is not the case. As Trudgill (2011) points out, even though Standard English is the variety used in writing, and associated with education, 'most native speakers of English in the world are native speakers of some nonstandard variety of the language'(2011, p. 2). Standard English is simply one of the many varieties of English; 'Standard English is a purely social dialect' (Trudgill, 2011, p. 8), but it is associated with 'power, wealth and prestige' (Trudgill, 2011, p. 9).

Nevertheless, researchers have examined witness testimony in courtrooms, paying attention to particular features, in order to determine whether language has an effect on credibility.

Activity 6.1

Look at the following exchanges between lawyers and witnesses. Are some more convincing than others? Why?

1. Lawyer: How well do you know the defendant?
   Witness: Well, I kinda met him years back you know?
2. Lawyer: Where were you standing that night?
   Witness: I was right across the street, approximately ten metres away.
3. Lawyer: What did you hear?
   Witness: It was sort of like a bang? Like a really loud bang noise.

A research project in the 1970s (O'Barr, 1982; O'Barr and Atkins, 1980) examined the language of witnesses, paying attention to the features that Robin Lakoff (1975) had suggested might be stereotypically associated with women's speech. These features included hedges, tag questions, rising intonation and empty adjectives. Looking at courtroom data, it was found that these features were not distributed according to sex (O'Barr, 1982). Because of this, it was suggested that these features are typical of 'powerless' language (see also Di Paolo and Green, 1990; Wodak, 1985).

The argument is that testimony including powerless features is less likely to be convincing to a jury. To test this, 'mock juries' were asked to listen to and rate recordings; some included features of powerful language and others contained instances of powerless language. All the examples were based on real testimony. Of the examples given in Activity 6.1, 1 and 3 have features of powerless language, while 2 is an example of powerful language. However, care needs to be taken, especially in the evaluation of short segments (Kerr Thompson, 2002) and in relation to any generalisations made about them. As Kerr Thompson points out, 'the outcome of trials is dependent, transparently, not just upon the language style of one witness, but on myriad factors' (2002, p. 159). Moreover, to focus on discrete linguistic features out of context suggests that each feature has only one function. For example, in Chapter 4 it was observed that speakers should not breach the maxim of quality. Hedging ('kind of', 'sort of') is an important way of ensuring that there is no such breach. This may be crucial in the context of the particular facts of the case, the questions that follow and what other witnesses say. Nevertheless, some witnesses do have less power than others in the court. But it is important to see that this is not just related to the presence or absence of a particular feature.

Aboriginal English

Discrimination on all kinds of grounds can occur in all kinds of places. In the courtroom, however, there are at least two things worth bearing in mind. First, the courtroom has its own rules of interaction which need to be followed (see Chapter 5). Second, the consequences of linguistic discrimination in the courtroom can be extremely severe. In the following, a variety of English is considered, one that could be called 'powerless' in so far as the rules that structure this language are very different from the interactional rules of the courtroom.

Activity 6.2

The following is a short extract from a cross-examination. Is the witness credible? DC is Defence Counsel and W is the Witness and = indicates a latch, when there is no gap and no overlap between speakers. Capitals indicate increased volume and underlining denotes emphasis.

1. DC: and you <u>knew</u> (1.4) when you spoke to these six police in the Valley that you didn't have to go anywhere with them if you didn't want to, didn't you?
2. W: (1.3) No.
3. DC: You <u>knew</u> that, Mr (1.2) Coley I'd suggest to you, please do not lie. you knew that you didn't have to go anywhere if you didn't want to, didn't you? (2.2) Didn't you? (2.2) Didn't you, Mr Coley.
4. W: (1.3) Yea.
5. DC: WHY DID YOU JUST LIE TO ME? WHY DID YOU JUST SAY NO MR COLEY? (4.4) YOU WANT ME TO SUGGEST A REASON MR COLEY? THE REASON WAS THIS, THAT YOU WANTED THE COURT TO <u>BELIEVE</u> (2.1) THAT YOU THOUGHT YOU HAD TO <u>GO</u> WITH POLICE, ISN'T THAT SO?

6. W: (1.2) Yeh.
7. DC: AND YOU <u>LIED</u> TO THE COURT, TRYING TO TO (1.2) YOU <u>LIED</u> TO THE COURT TRYING TO PUT ONE <u>OVER</u> ON THE COURT, DIDN'T YOU?
8. W: (1.8) (p) No.
9. DC: THAT WAS YOUR REASON, MR COLEY WASN'T IT? (3.1) WASN'T IT? (3.2) WASN'T IT, MR. COLEY?
10. W: (1.9) Yep=.
11. DC: =YES, (2.9) BECAUSE YOU WANTED THE <u>COURT</u> TO <u>THINK</u> THAT <u>YOU</u> DIDN'T KNOW THAT YOU COULD TELL THESE POLICE YOU WEREN'T GOING <u>ANY</u>WHERE WITH THEM. THAT WAS THE REASON WASN'T IT? (1.5) WASN'T IT?
12. W: (0.6) Yes=.
13. DC: =Yes.

(Eades, 2002, p. 171)

There are a few features here that may make the lawyer's arguments seem convincing. The witness seems to change his story; first saying 'no' in line 2 but changing this to 'yes' in line 4. The silences from the lawyer along with the repeated requests for answers may also suggest that the witness is reluctant to answer (see Chapter 5).

However, to understand what is going on, it is necessary to know something about the sociolinguistic rules of Australian Aboriginal English (AAE), which is the mother tongue of this witness. These inter-action rules relate to sociolinguistic competence. Part of knowing a language is being familiar with the syntactic, semantic and phonolog-ical structure of a language. Sociolinguistic competence, however, is about how to *do* things with language, over and above the basic struc-ture of a language. This concept allows consideration of the 'rules' followed when doing things like greeting someone, making requests, asking questions or engaging in small talk.

There are two interactional norms in AAE that are particularly important for this extract; they relate to silence and question forms (Eades, 2003, p. 202). In AAE, silence after a question is normal and is valued. Silence indicates that the person is taking the question seri-ously and it is particularly common in formal and semi-formal situ-ations. Silence signals neither reluctance to answer nor an inability to answer. Moreover, silence in Aboriginal culture is related to the way that speakers of AAE seek information. While in Standard

Australian English it is quite normal to ask questions with tags ('isn't it?', 'don't you?') or by inverting subject and object, in AAE it is much more usual to ask a question with a declarative. Finally, there is a phenomenon in AAE called 'gratuitous concurrence' (see Cooke, 1996; Eades, 1996). This means that speakers are very likely to answer 'yes' to some questions, regardless of what the 'true' answer is. This is much more likely to happen when questions are asked forcefully, either through increased volume and emphasis, by repetition or simply because the questioner has some kind of power over the addressee.

All of this is related to a particular knowledge economy in Australian Aboriginal culture. In Western culture generally, people are expected to share what they know. If someone is asked a question, a prompt, true and appropriate answer is the normal response (see Chapter 4). In Australian Aboriginal culture, information is precious; there are some pieces of knowledge that cannot be generally shared. What a particular person can be told depends on the relationship that exists between speaker and hearer (Eades, 1996). Thus, information seeking is often done 'indirectly as part of interaction in ongoing reciprocal relationships' (Eades, 2003, p. 202). The witness in Activity 6.2 may not have seen this lawyer before; to say they have a relationship is to stretch the normal meaning of that term.

Activity 6.3

Go back to the extract in Activity 6.2. Is it possible to interpret it differently given the rules of AAE?

In the light of the rules of AAE, the witness's responses now tell another story. It might also help to know that this is a young person, only 15 years old. Moreover, the case from which these lines are taken depended precisely on how demands from people with authority (the police) were understood by the witness. The nature of police requests have already been examined (Chapters 3 and 4). Imagine how much more forceful such a request would appear to a young adult. Note also that the force of authority is also clearly present in the lawyer's questions to the witness. The change of answer that the witness provides (line 2 as compared to line 4) can be understood as excellent evidence for the story the witness first gives; that he thought he had to comply with the request from the police officer.

- Sociolinguistic competence is about knowing how to do things with language.
- The rules of sociolinguistic competence vary between languages and language varieties.
- To understand power in the courtroom, looking at individual features of talk is not enough.

More than one silence

Diana Eades has conducted a great deal of research on Aboriginal English in a legal context, as well as working to improve understanding of it within the legal community in Australia. She notes that 'silence' is key for AAE speakers in a legal context, not only with respect to the way that AAE speakers may use silence, but also in relation to the way that such speakers are silenced by the court. Thus, she treats 'silence' as both a noun and a verb (Eades, 2000). Eades (2000) argues that this silencing may contribute to the high number of indigenous Australians in prison or in police custody. Here, it is important to remember that an individual's ethnicity is not determinative of their language variety (see also Chapter 7). Some indigenous Australians do not have AAE as a mother tongue, and others are bicultural and, hence, bilingual (see Eades, 2000). Obviously, individuals who are fluent in Standard Australian English, including the necessary sociolinguistic competence, may not experience the same kind of discrimination and silencing that AAE speakers do.

Activity 6.4

The following is an extract of examination-in-chief during a sentencing hearing. The witness assaulted one of the Smiths. Identify instances of silence (as noun and verb) in the following. DC is the Defence Counsel, the witness's lawyer. W is the witness and J is the Judge. The square bracket [shows where simultaneous talk begins.

285. DC: You go out of your way to avoid the Smiths?
286. W: (3.7) Well I stay out on the Reserve they stay over west and they come

```
                  [out there
287. J:           [Sorry
288. DC:          [Nice and    [slow
289. J:                        [You're going to have speak more slowly and
distinctly because     [I can't understand
290. WL:                       [ I stay out at the Reserve at East Mapletown and
the Smiths stay over at the west side of town – and they come out there
regularly out to the Reserve out to where I stay=
291. J: =I can't hear what you're saying and I  [don't think it's an answer.
292. DC:                                        [She stays out there –
they come out there regularly=.
293. J: =I don't think it's an answer to the question – you were asked 'Do
you go out of your way to avoid meeting the Smiths now?'.
294. W: Well I try to but they come out there and we can't avoid one
another because it's only just a little reserve.
```

(Eades, 2000, p. 175)

Interruptions are a standard way of silencing someone in a conversation. The witness seems to be interrupted at lines 287 and 291 as it is not clear that she has finished her turn. The witness is further silenced at line 291, when the judge explains that he doesn't think the witness is answering the question. At this point, the lawyer starts speaking for the witness. The judge makes his confusion clear, providing a metalinguistic comment on the interaction (line 291), and then, in line 293, he repeats the question. The preferred answer here, from the form of the question and from the context of the talk, is clearly 'yes' (Eades, 2000, p. 176). But when the witness finally gets her point across, in line 294, it becomes clear that she *was* trying to answer the question. Given where she lives it is simply not possible to avoid the Smiths. The witness was trying to give the court the necessary background information; she was trying to obey relevant Gricean maxims. Indeed, the silence at the start of her turn in line 286 suggests that she is taking the question seriously and thinking about a response. Further, use of the discourse marker 'Well' here is indicative of the speaker answering but being aware that she is not providing the preferred answer (Pomerantz, 1984).

In other instances that Eades has examined, the witnesses say very little (2000, p. 163). Sometimes this has to do with the way questions are put. In Chapter 5, questions were ranked in terms of how 'coercive' they are. But this coercion relies on rules that may not be shared by all speech communities. Thus, for AAE speakers, a declarative with rising intonation is a good, non-coercive, way of asking a question. There seems to be an example of this in line 285. While this might be seen to be constraining for other witnesses, in that it suggests a 'yes/no' answer, it fits well with AAE communicative norms. Eades (2000) also points out that when unproblematic information is being sought by a lawyer, that is, information that has already been accepted by the participants in the court, it can make sense for this to be offered in full by the lawyer, with the lawyer simply asking for a witness's agreement. Such parts of evidence may go on for some time, with the lawyer offering a string of declaratives with rising intonation and the witness agreeing. Eades calls this 'evidentiary harmony' to point out that, while the form of the question may look constraining, attention needs to be paid to what is going on in the stretches of talk under examination (see Chapter 5 on Shipman).

The different sociolinguistic competence required for AAE speakers means that speakers of this variety are at a real disadvantage in the courtroom. The rules of interaction in the courtroom clash with the rules of interaction of their language. The fact that AAE is a variety of English makes this disadvantage even more acute as the other participants may be oblivious to the existence of a second language in the courtroom. When the presence of another language is clear, however, other issues arise.

- When rules of interaction clash, discrimination and injustice are likely to occur.
- This is more likely with 'non-Standard' varieties of English or varieties demanding different sociolinguistic competence.

Moving between languages

Access to the law and to justice depends on access to the language of the law. The availability of interpreting in the legal context is an important right; in the courtroom, the fairness of a trial depends on good interpretation (Namakula, 2012; van der Vlis, 2010). It is worth noting at the outset that use of professional interpreters is not universal, and all kinds of people find themselves fulfilling the role of interpreter. While some settings demand a particular qualification, it is not uncommon for interpreters to be children, community members or

police officers (Hale, 2010, p. 441). In the following, I con\
preting in the courtroom. However, interpreting takes plac\
places; during arrest, detention and questioning by the p\
example, and these events will certainly inform what happei   ⟂ne
court (see Berk-Seligson, 2000, 2002; Eades, 2003).

The rules of speaking in court have already been considered (Chapter 5), but it helps to know something about translation and interpreting. I will make a distinction between translation and interpreting; but when discussing interpreting the terms will be used interchangeably. Translation usually refers to written texts. The translator takes a piece of writing in L1 (the source language) and translates it to L2 (the target language). While translators often work under time pressures, they are able to consult dictionaries, make use of translation software, and revise and redraft their work. Generally, they are also able to see the whole text that needs to be translated. Interpreters, on the other hand, work with spoken language.

There are two kinds of interpreting: consecutive and simultaneous. Simultaneous interpreting means that two people are talking at the same time. Of course, there has to be some delay between the speaker starting to talk and the interpreter beginning to speak, but the interpreter in simultaneous interpreting is doing two things at once; listening to a speaker in L1 and producing speech in L2. It is a very demanding mode of interpreting. Consecutive interpreting is also demanding, but at least only one person speaks at a time. For this to work well, the first speaker needs to provide enough speech for the interpreter to be able to make sense of the message, without it being too long to hold in working memory. Both modes of interpreting are challenging. In the context of the courtroom, especially, other challenges present themselves.

Activity 6.5

Think back to what we covered in Chapter 5 about rules of interaction in the courtroom. Consider also the ideologies that the law holds about language (Chapter 4). What effects might these factors have on a court interpreter? What other kind of practical issues might the interpreter have to deal with?

Chapter 4 showed that the linguistic ideology operating in the law suggests that language is objective and transparent. This is relevant to multilingual legal contexts as 'Jurists often consider interpreters as a "translation machine" that simply has to translate everything that is being said' (van der Vlis, 2010, p. 31; see also Hale, 2010, p. 441). This is a version of what is called the conduit model of communication (Reddy, 1979). The conduit model sees communication as a simple transmission of information from A to B (Chapter 1). This is hardly an accurate model, even when dealing with communication in a single common language; when two languages are involved it becomes even less convincing.

In addition to the general difficulties of interpreting, particular difficulties may arise because of the specific languages involved. For example, in German, 'ja' means 'yes' but it is also used as a filler or discourse marker, much like 'um' in English. In the Nuremberg trials, the interpreters had consistently been translating the German 'ja' as 'yes' (Karton, 2008, p. 3). Thus, a hesitation was transformed into assent. Moreover, some languages must specify information that is not required in English and vice versa.

Example 6.1

'Se me cayó en las escaleras'
Literal translation: 'To-me-it-happened that she fell on the stairs'.
(Filipovic, 2007, p. 262)

Filipovic shows that the translations given ('I dropped her' and 'she fell') caused confusion, as the same question was asked nine times; further 'by the end of the interview it was not clear from the translation whether the suspect was stating that he had dropped the victim voluntarily or involuntarily' (Filipovic, 2007, p. 262; see also Hale, 2010, p. 448). Intentionality is at issue here; and this is crucial in criminal law.

Interpreting from one language to another also requires knowing the legal language of both codes, as well as the language used by police, lawyers and judges (Hale, 2010). Legal language is, of course, closely related to legal structure, and not all places have the same legal system. Thus, it is possible that there simply will not be a good translation for much of this technical language. Likewise, terms which exist in normal English but have a special meaning in legal English may be prone to misinterpretation.

Example 6.2

Judge: Do you waive further notice of this date?

Spanish Interpreter: *¿Ud despide que se le deje saber de otras informaciones en este caso?* [Do you wave [good-bye] to receiving other information about this case?]

(DeJongh, 1992, p. 29)

Note also that the interpreter might well be perceived as akin to an expert witness (Chapter 7) and, thus, may be treated with some suspicion. It may be that the interpreter is the only person in the room who can understand the witness's language; other participants simply have to trust that what is being communicated is actually what the witness said. However, far from being fully briefed, the interpreter may not have been given any information about the case, the charge or the witness's testimony. Thus, they have no context at all for what they are hearing. On the one hand, this might seem to be a positive thing; the interpreter can then have no preconceptions. However, the kinds of choices that the interpreter has to make when moving from the source to the target language are made much more difficult by the absence of any context at all. Because of the rules of speaking that apply in a courtroom, the interpreter is also unlikely to be able to ask the witness (or the lawyer) for clarification. Certainly, a thorough understanding of professional ethics for interpreters in a legal context may help them determine when it is appropriate to seek clarification or explain an issue to the court (Hale, 2010).

Because of the communicative context, there are also practical matters that should be considered (Hale, 2010; Morris, 1999; Namakula, 2012). In terms of physical context, the interpreter may not even be present in the room, having to work down a telephone line (Kredens and Morris, 2010). Whether co-present or not, speakers should speak clearly, pausing regularly to allow the interpretation to take place. The interpreter also needs to be situated in a place where she can hear what is being said. She should be allowed to ask for clarification, to take notes, to have breaks and to have something to drink

(Hale, 2010). These things are not always provided. However, in courts which are routinely multilingual, interpreters are provided with separate sound proof booths, back-up interpreters and a 'monitor' – another interpreter – to check the interpretation as it occurs (Karton, 2008). Finally, an interpreter will be talking more than anyone in the courtroom, as they have to repeat everything that everyone says. 'Interpretation is an intense, exhausting activity' (Karton, 2008, p. 30). Because of all of these difficulties, detailed suggestions have been made to 'raise the bar' on legal interpreting. Hale urges recognition of the fact that interpreters are highly trained professionals who should have good training, 'adequate working conditions and [be paid] professional rates that are commensurate with the difficulty of the task' (Hale, 2010, p. 440).

- Differences between the structure and semantics of languages are difficult to manage.
- Interpreters face practical difficulties because of the rules and routines of the court.

Details, details

In the move from one language to another, interpreters will usually do two things: leave some elements out and add some elements in. At first glance this might suggest that interpreters are not very good at their job. It is important to understand that additions and deletions are often a necessary effect of the move from one language to another. There is no such thing as a 'perfect' translation. I will now consider some of the elements that are left out and added. They might not seem very important at first, but close consideration indicates otherwise.

Three features will be examined here: hedges, fillers and discourse markers. As already seen, a hedge is something that reduces the certainty or force of a statement. In the court especially, the level of commitment to something can be very important. It is not the case that certainty is always better than some careful and truthful hedging. Fillers, something used to fill a pause like 'uhm' or 'ah' may also have the effect of hedging. They can also indicate the presence of a sensitive or embarrassing topic. Finally, discourse markers serve a number of functions; examples include 'well', 'so' and 'still'. They structure utterances and arguments, and in this sense are the spoken equivalent of argument markers (like 'however', 'therefore' and so on). They can also provide particular kinds of information and emphasis.

The following examples come from Hale's work (2002) on the use of Spanish in courts in Sydney, Australia.

Example 6.3

Witness: Se me extravio. No se en realidad.
              (I lost it. I don't really know.)
Interpreter: I lost it.

(Hale, 2002, p. 31)

Here, uncertainty is removed as the 'I don't really know' part of the utterance is not communicated. The witness may now be held to this unqualified answer (Chapter 5). If the witness says anything which is at odds with the certainty of 'I lost it', the testimony may start to look un-credible.

Example 6.4

Answer: No, no se hablo de eso.
              (No, that wasn't discussed.)
Interpreter: I don't think so … I don't think so.

(Hale, 2002, p. 34)

In Example 6.4 we see the opposite of what happened in Example 6.3. Here, an answer which was unequivocal is made less certain by the interpreter.

Hale's data (2002) shows clearly that in the move from Spanish to English, the number of hedges, fillers and discourse markers went down and the number of hesitations went up. However, as Hale points out, this does not mean that all the original hesitations were included in the English version. And while there were fewer discourse markers overall in the English versions, this does not mean they were in the same place. Here, a couple of examples of the use of 'bueno', a discourse marker in Spanish, are examined. Hale identifies seven functions for 'bueno', and finds that it is often left out of the English translation.

Example 6.5

Question: Yeah, now, tell us what happened when you got home and found
            your husband packing up his clothes.
Answer: **Bueno**, ahi yo senti que mi matrimonio se … se terminaba todo, y
            bueno, yo fui la culpable porque con la rabia que tenia ah … tome
            el telefono en mi mano derecha y lo voltee contra … el velador.
            (Well, I felt then that my marriage was … was over, anyhow, it was
            my fault because I was so furious that uh I took the telephone with
            my right hand and smashed it against the … the lamp).
Interpreter: I was uh in fault, at fault because I was angry, very angry and on
            my anger I got the telephone on my hand and I banged it against
            the uh side table.

                                                                (Hale, 2002, p. 36)

Both uses of 'bueno' here are absent in the final version. The Spanish
speaker uses 'bueno' to signal the start of a narrative; this is one of the
functions of this discourse marker. While a narrative is produced in the
English version, in so far as there are two events temporally connected
(taking the telephone and banging it) the crucial 'justification' of this –
the realisation that her marriage was over – is missing. The hesitations
in the witness's answer appear also to have been deleted.

Recall that overall in Hale's data the number of hesitations went up.
This might be because hesitations are inserted where the interpreter is
having difficulty in finding a formulation, when the interpreter is
thinking or before a self-correction of some kind (Hale, 2002, p. 40).
Here, however, the witness's first hesitation may well be related to the
difficulty of realising that her marriage was over and thus it is important in understanding the material that follows. If looked at in this way,
the hesitation from the witness is evidence of emotional distress. This
distress is not present in the English version because an important part
of her testimony has been erased.

This example shows the importance of accuracy; related to this,
however, are issues of style. In another study, Hale found that interpreters tend to use a formal register in English, regardless of style of the
original (Hale, 1997, p. 204); this may well alter the court's perception
of a speaker's character.

Hale notes: 'the interpreter's immediate impulse is to bridge the
discursive gap between the law and the lay witness …' (1997, p. 208).

For this gap to be properly managed in legal contexts, the process of interpretation needs to be understood. First, especially in the case of interpretation, it is important to properly question the conduit model of communication (see Morris, 1999). Second, communication would be improved, and thus justice may be better served, if judges, lawyers and juries were fully aware of the particular difficulties that interpreters face. Allowing interpreters to take their time, to take notes or to have some access to witness statements may not seem like big changes, but they would make interpreters' work slightly less impossible.

Which language?

There is one more issue that needs to be considered. I have been treating the choice of language as unproblematic. But which language is appropriate is not always clear; thus, people may be spoken to in a language they are not fluent in. This may be because an appropriate interpreter is unavailable or because the interviewee seems able to understand and communicate in the language being used. Evidence gathered in this way, or testimony elicited from such a speaker, may be unreliable because of the difficulty they are having with the language. Thus, it is important to be sure that the interviewee really is as skilled in a language as they seem to be (or claim to be) (English, 2010).

Activity 6.6

Consider the following:

P: Right. Now I want to ask you some questions about the trouble out there but I want you to understand that you don't have to answer any questions at all. Do you understand that?
W: Yes.
P: Do you have to tell me that story?
W: Yes.
P: Do you have to though?
W: Yes.
P: Do you, am I making you tell me the story?
W: Yes.

> P: Or are you telling me because you want to?
> W: Yes.
>
> (Coldrey, 1987, pp. 84–5, cited in Gibbons, 2003, p. 209)
>
> What might be going on here?

This turns out to be a very clear example of gratuitous concurrence from a speaker of AAE. But such an exchange could also easily occur with a non-native speaker of English. If the police officer had stopped with the first question, and not gone on to check the witness's comprehension, the witness's difficulty may not have come to light. Even so, without understanding that there is such a thing as gratuitous concurrence, a questioner may conclude that the witness is being uncooperative.

Compare the extract in Activity 6.6 with the following example:

Example 6.6

Police: Which man, which man had this shining thing?
Witness: Who wear white thing.
Police: The white thing?
Witness: White, white shirt.
Police   Is he the man you stabbed in the backside?
Witness: Yeah.
Police: Yeah?
Witness: Yeah.
Police: And how long was this shining thing?
Witness: Fifteen second it's.
Police: How, how how?
Witness: Five seconds. How long? Ah yeah [responding to Police officer's gesture], I can't remember.
Police: You can't remember?
Witness: I see something shining but I can't remember.

(English, 2010, pp. 424–5)

This is clearly a witness struggling with the English language. Even so, at another point in the interview, the following exchange takes place.

Example 6.7

Police: My friend, my friend, this interview we've spoke now for an hour and
          a half.
Witness: Yeah.
Police: And you've spoken perfect English.
Witness: Yeah.

(English, 2010, p. 424)

Fiona English (2010) details how important it is for detainees to understand the language which is being used to interview them (see also Brière, 1978; Pavlenko, 2008). However, because of exchanges like the one in Example 6.7, it is likely that the detainee's proficiency will never be examined. English provides a methodology which can be used to assess language ability, paying attention not only to pronunciation and syntactic competence, but also to sociolinguistic competence. Engaging the detainee in conversation, using carefully chosen materials such as pictures of places which may be familiar or texts from their local newspapers, allows a language expert to fully assess linguistic competence. English suggests that audio materials should also be used and explains how to involve the 'testee' in collaborative communication to lessen the 'test effect'. In response to the objection that detainees may 'underperform' in these assessments, English's experience suggests that this is rare as 'it is quite a difficult thing to maintain throughout an extended face-to-face interview' (2010, p. 428). Indeed:

> What tends to happen is that a test effect comes into play and the detainee, caught up in the assessment process, strives to do well. Evidence of this might include expressions of irritation at not 'getting' something during a listening comprehension task, requests for an extract to be played again or attempts to seek the appropriate word during a discussion task (English, 2010, p. 428).

The assessor must balance all the evidence to construct an accurate profile of the person's linguistic ability. While a report can be provided for the court, the profile can also be used to examine the transcripts of the interviews with police that have already taken place in order to assess whether the detainee is likely to have understood the questions being asked.

This kind of assessment demonstrates the way in which existing methodologies for testing language proficiency can be useful for and adapted to legal contexts. For experts like English to be invited to conduct an assessment, however, depends on someone – the police, the individual's lawyers – realising that this is necessary.

- Interpreters may add or remove parts of a witness's utterance.
- This can have an effect on the witness's meaning and style.
- Interpreting is not always well understood by legal professionals.
- It may be necessary to fully assess an individual's linguistic proficiency.

Where are you from?

There is a lot that can be said about the treatment of asylum seekers in the legal process. As the focus in this chapter is multilingual contexts, I consider assessments of claims about origin based on the language the applicant speaks, as linguists may be involved in assisting with these assessments. When an individual seeks asylum, she may not have with her any documents to show where she is from. When fleeing from civil war or genocide, finding a passport and birth certificate is probably not a high priority. Establishing that an individual really does come from the region she claims to matters, as seeking asylum depends on having a 'well-founded fear of being persecuted for reasons of race, religion, nationality, membership of a particular social group or political opinion' (United Nations, 1951). People with partic- ular religious beliefs are persecuted in some parts of the world but are protected in others.

There has been a great deal of discussion and debate about the role of linguists and the role of native speakers in making these assess- ments (Eades, 2005, 2010; Fraser, 2009; Language and National Origin Group, 2004). In any case, for assessments like this there are two parts. First, the variety of language that the individual is using needs to be identified. This may include identifying the dialect or accent and establishing whether a single dialect is used or whether there is some mixing of varieties. Second, in the case of asylum claims, this has to be geographically located. The language of the individual and the geographical distribution of this language both need to be considered.

The relationship between language and geography might seem straightforward. In the West and in Northern Europe, it is normal to think about languages as being related to national borders. For example, in France people speak French. But in many parts of the world, languages are not confined to well-marked out national borders. (This is true even of France, where Basque and Breton are both spoken.) Moreover, as Fraser notes, asylum seekers 'often come from regions characterised by complex multilingualism, creolisation or diglossia, [regions] which have had little attention from linguistic science' (2009, p. 128). In short, very little may be known about the link between a region and its languages. Further, it is entirely possible that a person lives in an area, and has lived there for many years, without having the linguistic features of a 'typical' inhabitant. Someone who moved from Scotland to Germany in their 20s and then lived there for 40 years may still have the accent of a non-native speaker of German.

Finally, asylum seekers do not always move quickly and directly from point A to point B. The journey which ends in an asylum application may well last for many years, involving periods in refugee camps and in other countries. Indeed, this can be useful if looked at in the right way, as these movements may well leave linguistic traces which can then be used to confirm what an individual has said about the journey from their place of origin to the nation in which they seek asylum. But, without proper attention to the kinds of long and complex journeys which asylum seekers may undertake, evidence of other languages and varieties may well be interpreted as contradicting claims about where an individual is originally from (see Blommaert, 2001, 2009).

- Linguists are involved in determining individuals' geographical origin.
- Understanding multilingual contexts and the journeys of asylum seekers is important in making these determinations.

Conclusion

When the issues around interpreting and identifying languages are acknowledged, the problems and potential difficulties become very clear. However, because people tend to think of themselves as experts in their own language, they may not pause to do this kind of analysis.

Trying to change someone's ideologies and assumptions in any area can be difficult enough; trying to alter them in relation to a topic in which they consider themselves expert may be impossible. Realising that everyone has preconceptions about language may help in some ways; at least this makes clear that all people have beliefs which inform their thinking about language and communication. Indeed, even linguists have their own ideologies about language (Cameron, 1995). While ideologies about language can never be completely eliminated, it is important to try and counter the negative effects they may have in a legal context.

7

The CSI effect?

In this chapter, the contribution linguists make in analysing spoken evidence will be examined. I want to begin by examining some of the preconceptions people have about evidence by outlining the 'CSI effect'. Watching television dramas like CSI suggests that physical evidence has only one story to tell. The reality is rather more complex. CSI (Crime Scene Investigation) dramas have been set in a number of American cities. They focus on the work of crime scene investigators, who collect and analyse anything from the saliva on a cigarette butt to the presence of a rare fibre. These dramas have arguably had some effect on the trying of cases, and there has been a great deal of specu-lation, anecdotal evidence and now a growing body of research around what is known as the CSI effect (Cole and Dioso-Villa, 2009; Schweitzer and Sacks, 2007; Shelton et al., 2007).

There are actually three CSI effects. The first is that criminals may have become better at removing evidence of their crimes due to knowledge gained by watching these dramas. The second is that juries may now expect the kind of forensic evidence they are used to seeing on television shows. Without the truth-telling fibre, blood sample or epithelial tissue the jury may doubt the prosecution's case. The third CSI effect also relates to the jury. It has been suggested they may now have more confidence in their own ability to assess forensic evidence and are thus more likely to doubt experts. This may be especially true when juries are confronted with real forensic experts who do not talk about 'matches', and who are clear about what the evidence can say and what it cannot.

Dramas like CSI depend on a clear message; 'the evidence doesn't lie'. This suggests that physical evidence is conclusive and there is only ever one 'truth' that it tells. However, this singular interpretation is not what actually happens. A real-life crime scene investigator says, 'We never use the word "match"' about two samples. He continues:

The terminology is very important. On TV, they always like to say words like 'match,' but we say 'similar,' or 'could have come from' or 'is associated with'. (Toobin, 2007)

The same is true for linguists. When dealing with specific samples of written or spoken language, it is rarely possible to come to a definitive conclusion. Nevertheless, there is a great deal that linguists can do with samples of language. In this chapter and the next, the work that forensic linguists undertake is explored. Working with spoken and written texts, forensic linguists try to identify and profile speakers and authors, assist in investigations and then testify about their work in court. In this chapter, the focus is spoken material, while written texts are covered in the next chapter. Towards the end of this chapter, I also outline some of the issues that the expert linguist has to deal with when presenting evidence.

Three ways to find a speaker

When working with spoken data, the linguist's task is generally to try and identify the speaker. Broadly speaking, this can be done in one of three ways (Watt, 2010). The first is lay speaker identification; this includes the role of the 'earwitness'. Anyone can become a witness to a crime by hearing something (but not seeing who said it). The task of the earwitness is to help identify the speaker. I will cover the reliability of earwitnesses later in this chapter. The second mode of speaker identification involves analysis by a linguistic expert. Forensic phoneticians are highly trained linguists who are able to hear, detect and document even tiny features of someone's speech. The third mode of speaker identification is automatic, and relies on technology (Watt, 2010). While automatic identification will not be covered here, it will become clear during this chapter that the nature of human voices means that this kind of technology is not as useful in speaker identification as one might think.

As highly trained experts in human voice and sound, there are a number of things that forensic phoneticians can do (French, 1994). They can assist in profiling unknown speakers, help determine whether a suspect produced a spoken text (speaker identification) and put together 'voice line-ups' for earwitnesses to listen to. They can also assist in evaluating and applying the evidence of earwitnesses by, for example, drawing on work that helps translate into linguistic terms how people describe language in lay terms. Forensic phoneticians can also help to clarify unclear recordings. For example, the following may sound very similar, even though they mean very different things.

Example 7.1

I'm going to bomb out this place.
I'm going to bump out this place.

(A 'bump out' is a minor modification to a house). A phonetician might be asked to analyse a recording and say which of the two utterances in Example 7.1 was produced. There is a rather complex example of this kind of analysis at the end of the chapter.

Over and above speaker identification and profiling, forensic phoneticians can also give a judgement on whether a recording has been tampered with (French, 1994), whether utterances were recorded in the same place (based on acoustics of the space or background noise), whether utterances or speakers have been added to a recording or whether the order of utterances has been changed. They can also assist with non-speech sounds, like coughing. In a case of suspected cheating on the game show 'Who Wants to Be a Millionaire', forensic linguists were called in to help identify a cougher and to assess whether these coughs were being used to prompt the contestant (French and Harrison, 2004).

In short, the task of the forensic phonetician is the detail of sound. Phoneticians' skills and training mean they can make fine distinctions between sounds – even sounds from the same speaker. The following example is a straightforward case for a phonetician, as it does not even involve listening to recordings, but it is a nice example of the importance of the detail of sound.

It's my word!

Intellectual property is a valuable thing. Whether it relates to a particular manufacturing process, a recipe or musical compositions, this form of – very often intangible – property is protected by the law.

Trademarks are a particular kind of intellectual property, and are often important for a product or company's branding. It is, therefore, important for the trademark owner to reap all rewards from a brand that they have developed, as well as to protect the value of their brand by making sure that it is not being used by other people.

An American case provides a good example (*Aveda Corp.* v *Evita Marketing, Inc.,* 706 F. Supp. 1419, cited in Tiersma and Solan, 2002, p. 228). Aveda is an established brand in hair products. Evita started marketing a line of hair products with the brand name 'Avita'. Aveda were not happy and took Evita to court. Evidence was produced suggesting that consumers thought 'Aveda' and 'Avita' was the same thing. Evidence also indicated that Evita may be trying to capitalise on Aveda's established reputation. Evita were instructed to cease using the name (Tiersma and Solan, 2002, p. 228). In this case, a linguist provided evidence that 'Aveda' and 'Avita' are homophones for many people, especially in North America where these events took place. The court decided that the two were similar enough to cause consumer confusion.

Activity 7.1

Using a recorder and or a group of people, say 'Aveda' and 'Avita' (vary the order). Get other people to identify which is which. Try to just say them normally; that is, do not try to make them sound different; it might help to put them in a sentence, for example 'I love this Aveda/Avita product for my hair'. Is there confusion about which is which?

Many speakers of English will not produce or hear any difference between these two words; this is especially true in the US, where the case occurred. Even though the spelling is different, when spoken aloud, the two words could easily be confused with each other.

Making it clear

Just as the difference (or lack of difference) between particular phonemes can be important, who said what to whom may be very important in a legal context. But even with a recording of what was said, disputes arise. Working with a perfect recording – one that has been recorded in a space with little background noise, high quality equipment and people who are speaking clearly – is not common in any context, legal or otherwise. When covert recordings are taken for purposes of surveillance, microphones have to be placed in unobtrusive spaces; these may not be ideal for recording clear speech. In such instances, a forensic phonetician might be asked to clarify what is being said.

Activity 7.2

During a time when a number of people are present and talking, record the interaction. It is important that you get consent from the people in the room. Place the recording device somewhere unobtrusive. Once you have made a recording, see if you can transcribe some of the recording. How many times do you have to listen to it? How easy is it to tell who is talking? How easy is it to figure out what they are saying?

Background noise, multiple speakers or simply a low-quality recording make it difficult to establish what was actually said. Even in 'good' recording situations, like a police interview room, problems can arise (Bucholtz, 2000). In the case of surreptitious recording, subjects are certainly not aware of being recorded and so will not be trying to provide 'good data'.

Olsson reports being asked to clarify a recording which was taken covertly in a moving vehicle (2009, p. 155). The informant appeared to be talking about two people, 'Ernie' and 'Ronnie'. While police were aware of an 'Ernie' in connection with the case, 'Ronnie' was an entirely new person as far as the police were concerned. Using both auditory and acoustic methods (described in the next section) Olsson concluded that what sounded like 'Ronnie' was in fact 'Ernie'. He describes how the mishearing could easily have occurred, but argues that in this case such 'auditory confusion is only applicable to people who might be listening to the conversation as outsiders' (2009, p. 158). Indeed, the addressee of the Ronnie/Ernie utterances passed no comment at the time, suggesting that it was clear to him that 'Ernie' was the person being referred to throughout the interaction.

- Forensic phoneticians pay attention to the sounds of spoken language.
- There are a number of things they might be asked to do, from speaker identification to clarification of unclear recordings.
- The smallest detail of speech may be crucial in a legal case.

Listening, looking and measuring

In the Ernie/Ronnie case just discussed, Olsson used two approaches to the study of sound: the auditory and the acoustic. Both methods are highly specialised; in the following, an outline of these methods is given in order to appreciate the differences of these methods and thus show how they complement each other.

When speaking, people produce sound waves, and the form of these depends, to some extent at least, on the physical structure of a person's articulators (lips, tongue and teeth), as well as the character-istics of the vocal tract and resonating chambers (mouth, nose and so on). Speech can be considered as having two 'ends', the production end – what people do with their bodies – and the reception end – what another person hears. Paying attention to the reception end is called 'auditory' phonetics. It relies on repeated listening by an expert trained to hear the fine detail of human speech sound by sound, that is, phoneme by phoneme. Some of the differences heard may be relevant in identifying a speaker or establishing what someone said and some may not. For example, Olsson reports on a case where he was asked to form a judgement on whether a suspect had produced a particular utterance; a threat made over the telephone. Olsson notes that this requires consideration of three things. First, the analyst needs to estab-lish whether the two samples are 'apparently of the same dialect/accent'; second, 'are the voices of the same type' and, finally, is the 'pronunciation of certain speech sounds' the same (Olsson, 2009, pp. 41–2). Both samples Olsson was given were of the same dialect and had the same voice quality. Importantly, both the speaker of the threat and the suspect had a habit of pronouncing 'p' like 'b'; thus, both said what sounded like 'kneecabs', 'sbeak' and 'beriod'. Together with other similarities, Olsson concluded there was a 'high probability' that the suspect made the threat (2009, p. 43).

The auditory approach can also document intonation patterns and voice quality. Voice quality is described with terms like 'breathy' or 'creaky' (Olsson, 2009, p. 43), and it depends on what a speaker is doing with her vocal apparatus. Indeed, while the term 'voice quality' suggests that a speaker has a consistent 'quality' to her voice, this is not necessarily the case. Voice quality can change by the syllable and noticing this requires a particular kind of attention.

The auditory approach has historically been understood as a British tradition. Further, because this approach relies on an individual listening repeatedly and transcribing everything in great detail, it has also generally been thought of as more of an art than a science. However, this characterisation may have more to do with the differences of the auditory approach when compared to the acoustic.

The acoustic tradition has been associated with the USA and, as intimated, is sometimes thought to be more 'scientific' than the auditory method. This is because it is possible to 'measure' details of speech. Acoustic work pays attention to frequency, the speed of the sound waves produced in speech. For example, it is possible to assign a numerical value to someone's average fundamental frequency (F_0). The F_0 'gives rise to the impression of overall pitch height of a voice' (French, 1994, p. 177). However, a voice is comprised of more than one frequency. Other frequencies, which are harmonics superimposed on the F_0, are also examined by linguists (they are labelled F_1, F_2 and so on). While the F_0 is an important tool in acoustic analysis, it may shift, even for an individual. For example, people tend to raise their F_0 when speaking on the telephone (Hirson, French and Howard, 1995, cited in French, 1994).

The acoustic method pays close attention to the profile of the physical properties of the sound waves produced during speech. Visual representations of sound waves, spectrograms, can be produced, and numerical values established for various characteristics of the sound wave. Nevertheless, as French notes, 'similarities and differences revealed by such examinations are – and must be – subject to careful interpretation' (1994, p. 176). At the very least, the analyst may need some information about the recording context. For example, in addition to people raising their F_0 on the telephone, the telephone also cuts some vocal frequencies; knowing that a recording was taken from a telephone conversation is important information to have.

While the two approaches are different, in practice, they are generally used together. Nolan argues that 'The two forms of analysis are symbiotic' (2001, p. 11). When using the tools of acoustic analysis it helps to be able to narrow down which features need to be examined;

this can be done through the kind of listening that auditory experts engage in. Likewise, looking at spectrograms may help confirm or question what the auditory phonetician has heard. It is also important to know that even though two utterances may sound the same they may have a very different acoustic profile (French, 1994). While it is not possible to talk about 'voice fingerprints', when it comes to comparing a recorded sample with a restricted pool of suspects the linguistic evidence can be compelling.

- The analysis of voices can be done using auditory or acoustic methods.
- Their approaches and histories may differ but they are generally used together.

Fingerprinting a voice?

From watching CSI and Hollywood films, it is easy to think that there is such a thing as a voice fingerprint. Dramas sometimes show an analyst using a computer to analyse a recording. The computer then returns a 'match' with a voice that is 'on file'. In reality, voiceprints like this do not exist and exact matches are impossible. Thus, when a forensic expert provides evidence about speaker identification, it is always within a paradigm of uncertainty (Coulthard, 2004; French and Harrison, 2007; French et al., 2010; Nolan, 2001). That does not mean that it is always impossible to tell exactly who a speaker is; however, to do this usually requires some other kind of evidence. For example, surveillance recordings from a particular place and time may be available so that investigators know who was present when a recording was made. If there is no visual record of a subsequent conversation, a forensic linguist may be asked to help figure out who said what. The important detail here is that the linguist is dealing with a closed and known set of people. Deciding whether Tom, Dick or Harry – all known to be in the same place at the same time – produced a particular utterance is rather different from picking one of these men out of a group of all possible speakers.

   While people might like to think that their voices are unique and like a 'fingerprint', some activities help show that this is not the case.

Activity 7.3

For this activity, you will need a tape recorder or digital recorder (or a group of people) and some other items. First, record yourself speaking 'normally'. Then, try some of these voice manipulation techniques and assess the difference.

> Put a pencil in your mouth.
> Speak in a much higher/lower pitch than you normally would.
> Imitate someone, or someone else's variety. This is not about accuracy!
> Hold your nose.
> Put something like a mint under your tongue.

Doing this activity should make clear that voices change all the time. For example, when speaking to a known person on the telephone, it is usually possible to tell if she has a cold, or has just woken up. This shows that the sound of a voice can change. Nolan calls this 'plasticity'. 'The net result of this plasticity of the vocal organs is that no two utterances from the same individual are ever, strictly speaking, identical in a physical sense' (Nolan, 2001, p. 2).

The issue of speaker profiling and identification is further complicated by the ways some speakers can exploit their vocal plasticity. It has generally been thought that it is not possible for a non-native speaker of a dialect to be able to pass as a speaker of that variety. However, some people also appear to be so good at 'imitation' that they can pass as native (Evans, 2002, 2010). It is also possible for speakers to be native in more than one dialect (Purnell, Idsardi and Baugh, 1999). Finally, it is possible to disguise a voice, and there are even telephones on the market that claim to do this for you.

- Voice fingerprints do not exist.
- Voices have plasticity, which means even the same speaker can sound very different.

Painting a picture

Even though voice fingerprints do not exist, it is nevertheless possible to say something about who produced a spoken text. An expert can make an informed judgement about some voices.

Activity 7.4

What kinds of things could be said about an unknown speaker from a sample of their voice?

It is usually possible to assess the sex of a speaker, their age and perhaps something about their regional origin or even level of education. Speaker profiling might draw on other discourse features, or use of specific words and phrases associated with a region (Shuy, 2001). If the analyst is lucky, the unknown speaker may have a distinctive feature. For example, as 'only about 3 per cent of the population have any kind of stammer' this would be a valuable feature to find (Olsson, 2009, p. 44). Nevertheless, conclusions need to be carefully drawn, the terms used need to be chosen carefully.

Activity 7.5

Consider the following. You are on holiday in Denmark. You are British by birth, but as your mother is Danish and you have spent a great deal of time there, you are fluent in the language. A threatening phone call is made to the Prime Minister of Denmark. It is traced to a phone box right outside your hotel. You are the only person staying in the hotel who was not born and raised in Denmark. You are arrested on the basis that the Prime Minister's secretary reports that the voice on the phone 'sounded foreign' and you do not have an alibi for the time of the call. What might you say in your defence?

There are various questions raised by this scenario. What does it mean, for example, to 'sound foreign'? Would it not be argued that even though you are fluent in Danish it is within your power to affect a 'foreign accent'?

As I have said that linguists can profile a speaker, it is important to be clear about what this means, as 'profiling' in current use is often associated with discrimination. Of course, discrimination of this kind can occur as a result of linguistic profiling, but this is not a necessary connection. Here, I make a distinction between profiling a voice and a speaker. Imagine, for example, a threatening call made by a voice which falls into the frequency range normally associated with males. Common sense and indeed statistical information would suggest that the caller is a man. However, some women have deep voices that easily fall into this range.

This distinction will not be a problem for linguists familiar with the standards and demands of being an expert witness. But in the case of lay speaker identification it may be more difficult. It is made even more problematic in some jurisdictions because of court decisions. In *Clifford* v *Commonwealth* (1999; cited in Preston, 2009, p. 75), the Supreme Court of Kentucky allowed witness evidence asserting that a voice belonged to a person of a particular ethnicity. The court held that it was acceptable to allow evidence which claimed to

> identify a voice as being that of a particular race or nationality, so long as the witness is personally familiar with the general characteristics, accents, or speech patterns of the race or nationality in question, i.e., so long as the opinion is 'rationally based on the perception of the witness' (*Clifford* v *Commonwealth*, 1999).

The dissenting judge, Justice Stumbo, however, wrote 'I fail to see any rationality in the notion that one can hear a person's skin colour' (*Clifford* v *Commonwealth*, 1999), which puts the distinction made above between voices and speakers very starkly. Commenting on this case and taking into account linguistic research in the field, Dennis Preston suggests the following reformulation:

> Testimony may be allowed which suggests that lay persons can often identify a person's age, gender, ethnicity, social status, regional background and other demographic characteristics from voice alone so long as (1) the person making the identification is a member of the speech community within whose boundaries the identification in question is taking place; (2) the person who is being identified is an authentic speaker of the variety which would suggest that demographic identification; (3) the speaker was not trying to disguise his or her voice by imitating another variety of the language in question; and (4) there is no evidence that any well-known stereotype of speakers of the class being identified has led the witness to assume facts about the speaker's language which were not actually present. (Preston, 2009, p. 75)

When there is a witness to a spoken crime, there are things that can be done in order to help in the identification of the speaker. This brings me to the topic of voice line-ups.

- If enough is known about a variety, it may be possible to profile an unknown voice.
- Care must be taken to keep the voice profile and person profile separate.

Lining them up

In the case of an eyewitness who has seen a suspect, identification appears to be reasonably straightforward. A physical line-up can be put together and the witness asked to identify the person they saw. (This is not to suggest that eyewitnesses are completely reliable (Loftus, 1996; see Chapter 8)). In the case of voices, it is a bit harder.

As mentioned above, one of the things that forensic phoneticians can do is provide advice on the construction of a voice line-up. As the name suggests, this is an auditory version of the classic suspect line-up. Putting a voice line-up together is rather more time consuming than a physical line-up. However, in some cases, this may be a crucial part of the investigation. When conducted, it is important that the line-ups are constructed in such a way that they are not vulnerable to attack in court. I follow Nolan (2003) and look at the various steps involved in such a line-up and then examine how reliable earwitnesses are generally.

For a voice line-up to be robust, one first needs some recordings of voices. Obviously one of these will be the voice of the suspect. There also need to be other voices, which are called 'foils'. There has to be some similarity between the suspect and the foils and this should take into account a number of different features. The samples need to share some features related to voice quality, pitch, accent and so on; if they are very similar, however, this sets the bar for the earwitness too high.

Activity 7.6

Someone has been calling all the high school principals in the area with a bomb threat. A couple of people who received these calls recorded them. Based on some tip-offs and other information, the police now have a suspect and they want to construct a voice line-up. Before think-ing about the other voices, how would you get an appropriate sample of voice from the suspect? An interview with the police may have been recorded; but which parts might you choose?

An interview with the police will have many sections. There might be talk about very normal and mundane things, but there might also be talk which deals with criminal activity. This is something that the person constructing the voice line-up has to think about. Would it be fair, for example, to use the following from a suspect?

Example 7.2

I did not threaten to blow up the school!

There are a few problems with using such an extract. The first, and most obvious, is the content of the message. As it deals directly with a criminal act (albeit by way of denial), it may cause an earwitness to identify this person as the caller; not because they recognise the voice, but because of the content. Of course, it would be possible to get samples of the same utterance from other speakers so that every-one in the line-up is saying the same thing. However, care also needs to be taken with the interactional context. Imagine Example 7.2 is a police interview in which someone is being challenged about the legality of their behaviour. If this example were to be used, all the foils should match in this respect. If the suspect was angry, or upset or simply forceful in the utterance, this would have to be taken into account. That is, the samples all have to be interactionally similar. As a result, the recordings used in an actual line-up may simply be single words or phrases pasted together (Nolan, 2003, p. 279). The acoustics of the recording situation also need to be considered so that the suspect's sample doesn't 'stand out'. It would not be possible, for example, to record the foils in a quiet sound studio if the suspect recording was taken on a busy street. Finally, before the line-up is played to the actual witnesses, it should be trialled with people who have nothing to do with the case. That is, once a voice line-up has been put together, it is good practice to gather some people, ask them to listen to the line-up and report on who they think sounds 'guilty' (Nolan, 2003).

Putting a voice line-up together is not easy. While in some cases it might be very important, and useful, to get an earwitness response to a voice line-up, earwitness identification is problematic in another way. Specifically, people are not very good at remembering voices well enough to identify them later (Yarmey, 2003). Of course, this all depends on the individual and the particular voice being identified. It may also depend on the context of the 'witnessing'. Remembering a voice that, at the time, seemed to be talking about something completely mundane is probably rather difficult. Remembering the voice of someone who is clearly menacing for more than a short time may be easier. Indeed, Nolan reports that 'by becoming familiar with the voice in a stress-inducing situation or interacting with the speaker rather than just overhearing' improves earwitness results (Nolan, 2001, p. 5). In this case, however, the stress of the situation itself needs to be considered from another point of view; the hearer may be so upset that she does not remember much at all. Research also suggests that if people know they have to remember a voice they will be a bit better than if they had no notice; but levels of accurate identification are still very low (Yarmey, 2003).

There are some factors which seem to improve recollection (Watt, 2010). Familiarity with the voice helps. Thus, people are more likely to correctly identify a voice they already know well. As mentioned, if the voice is heard for a period of time, this may also help. The time that passes between hearing the voice and identifying it also has an effect. On the other hand, there are some things that make the task harder, including if the person is shouting or whispering. An earwitness being sure of their identification should also be treated with caution, as confidence does not correlate with accuracy (Yarmey, 2003).

It seems to be the case, then, that earwitness evidence is not particularly reliable. Yarmey cites Deffenbacher et al. (1989) approvingly:

> earwitnessing is so error prone as to suggest that no case should be prosecuted solely on identification evidence involving an unfamiliar voice (1989, p. 118, cited in Yarmey, 2003, p. 72).

This does not mean it should never be used, rather, it should be used carefully and in conjunction with other evidence (though see Liberty, 2003).

- Voice line-ups are complicated and time consuming to put together.
- They need to be carefully designed and tested.
- Earwitnesses are not particularly reliable.

Too clever for court

The work that forensic linguists do may be used in the investigative stages of a case. It may also be used in the trial itself, with the linguist being called as an expert witness in the trial. Linguists are called as experts in very different kinds of areas. I deal first with the issues that confront linguists undertaking speaker/author identification and profiling. The situation for other kinds of linguistic evidence is different, so this also needs to be addressed. I then move on to the way experts might be perceived by the courts and, finally, I turn to the challenge of presenting linguistic evidence to the court.

As there is no such thing as a voice fingerprint, the conclusions that linguists come to about speaker identification have to be phrased in a specific way. A number of British forensic linguistics authored a position statement which can be used by linguists in the preparation and presentation of their work. It sets out a two-stage assessment in judging whether two utterances have been made by the same person (French and Harrison, 2007). The first is whether the two are 'consistent', 'not consistent' or whether it's 'not possible to say'. If the two samples are 'consistent', an expert can then go on to say something about whether the speaker is 'distinctive' or not. The scale of judgements available ranges from finding that two samples are 'highly unlikely' to be the same to 'highly probable' that two samples are the same (Nolan, 2001). This scale, or something very similar, can also be used in cases of author identification for written texts. Nevertheless, the position statement is not 'set in stone' (French et al., 2010, p. 150) and it has been debated (Rose and Morrison, 2009).

There are matters about which linguists can be rather more certain. In the 1990s, the Oakland School Board published a resolution which acknowledged the existence of a variety of English, African American Vernacular English (AAVE) (Wolfram, 1998). It further resolved to teach students with AAVE as a mother tongue in a way that took into account the fact that Standard American English (SAE) was not their first language. But the resolution was widely misunderstood as claiming that AAVE was genetically determined, and that speakers of AAVE were less intelligent than their SAE speaking peers. In this case, linguists were able to explain what AAVE was and what the resolution meant. Uncertainty was not an issue here.

However, who was called to testify in the related Senate hearings is instructive. Wolfram notes that, in addition to two sociolinguistic experts, two non-linguists were allowed to testify. He compares this to 'two nonexperts arguing with two well-credentialed research physicists about the ramifications of a particular law of physics in industrial manufacturing' (1998, p. 111). This suggests that people have their own strongly held convictions about language and consider themselves experts in their own language variety (see Chapter 6). This presents a challenge for the expert linguist in court. In particular, the linguist is in a difficult position when it comes to expressing her evidence. If the language she uses is too 'ordinary' she 'risks having her evidence excluded as being nothing more than common sense ...' (Ainsworth, 2009, p. 285). At the same time, 'the expert who is too wedded to professional jargon and fully articulated theory may find her testimony excluded ... on the grounds that it may be confusing to the jury' (Ainsworth, 2009, p. 285; see also Coulthard, 1997; Tiersma and Solan, 2002).

Finally, the linguist is confronted with a number of practical and ethical issues (Ainsworth, 2009; Levi, 1994). Judges and lawyers may not trust experts for any number of reasons (Gray, 2010, p. 202). The first, paradoxically, is because legal professionals are not well informed about the areas in which expert witnesses are asked to testify. This is, of course, exactly why experts are needed. Second, there may be suspicion that experts are biased in favour of the party who has called them. Ainsworth notes that while the lawyer's job is to look after her client (2009, p. 283), the expert witness must be diligent and objective. But this is not always easy, especially as in preparing for a trial the expert may come to feel part of the legal team (Ainsworth, 2009, p. 284).

One solution

There are some practical solutions to the problems that expert linguists, and indeed all experts, face in court. Justice Gray (2010) of the Federal Court in Australia has outlined these issues and also described some of the remedies he has adopted in his courtroom. First, he makes sure that experts understand their role in the trial;

second, he brings the 'opposing' experts together before the trial. (Note that in some places, lawyers have to agree on a common expert.) This produces a statement which makes clear any points of difference between the experts. This is a good way of getting to the heart of the disagreement; it also helps the experts to explain their own findings in relation to their 'opponent' expert. Finally, Justice Gray provides the experts with a space in the trial proceedings to have a dialogue with each other about their points of difference. Only then are questions from lawyers and judges allowed. This last part of the process is called 'hot tubbing', and Justice Gray points out that it relies on the expertise of the witnesses and their mutual respect. It also seems to be informed by a less adversarial approach to expert witnesses, and he reports that anecdotal evidence suggests his approach is a positive improvement.

It is worth noting that, as important as expert witnesses are, they are not the final arbiters of fact; this job falls to the jury or the judge. While Tiersma and Solan note that there may be 'fear that linguistic expertise might usurp the role of the jury' (2002, p. 229), French and Harrison observe:

> Neither the speech scientist nor DNA scientist identifies the suspect. They provide the jury with the specialist information necessary to make the identification (or otherwise) themselves (2007, p. 138).

- Linguistic experts are not always welcomed by the courts.
- There are a number of ethical, practical and communicative issues the linguistic witness needs to manage.
- It is possible to change procedural rules in the court to make the battle of the experts less problematic.

Did you hear what he said?

I am going to finish this chapter with a case. It is an excellent example of just how difficult the work of forensic phoneticians can be and how much care is taken in assessing evidence.

David Bain was accused of murdering his family in New Zealand (Innes, 2011). He was found guilty and the case went to the Court of Appeal in New Zealand three times. The case finally went to the Privy Council (in the United Kingdom), who ordered a retrial. Part of the

evidence considered by the Crown and the defence, but never actually
played in court, was a call he made to the emergency services. Before
the retrial, a police detective reported that he heard words on the
emergency call that amounted to incriminating material. The individual who took the call was then asked to listen to the recording to see
what he could hear. A number of linguists were consulted about the
matter.

Activity 7.7

Go to http://tvnz.co.nz/david-bain-news/david-bain-s-111-call-made-
public-2718171/video
  Listen to this recording; especially the portion after the following
exchange (at about 23 seconds).

Bain: [heavy breathing audible] My [inaudible] family they're all
               dead hurry up.
Operator: It's okay Every St and it runs off off (1) Somerville St?
Bain: Yes.

Write down what you can hear in as much detail as possible. Compare
what you heard with your colleagues.

A number of expert forensic phoneticians from around the world were
asked to analyse and comment on this recording, specifically, to try
and ascertain what Bain had said in the disputed portion. While it was
not entirely clear that anything had been said at all, a number of utterances were suggested including, 'I shot the prick', 'I can't breathe', 'I
can't help puking' and 'I can't touch' (Rose, 2009). Did you hear any of
these? How certain are you that what you heard is what Bain said?
  The distinction made in the last two questions is very important. It
is entirely possible to hear something that was not said. There are a
number of reasons this may happen and sometimes a 'mishearing' can
be resolved as exactly that (by asking the interlocutor to repeat what
she said). What is interesting about the reports by linguists is that they
acknowledge that one could *hear* any number of words, but this does
not mean that this was what Bain had *said*. Thus, it is possible to
accept that the police detective did hear 'I shot the prick', as he
claimed, and still maintain that this is not what Bain actually said. One

of the experts, Philip Rose (2009), points out that unclear utterances tend to be processed 'top down' rather than working from the small details, which would be 'bottom up' processing. Another expert, French, put it as follows: 'If one were to draw an analogy with visual stimuli, we have all had the experience of seeing pictures in the cloud that arise from no more than coincidental arrangement of water particles' (cited in Innes, 2011, p. 148).

There was a great deal of debate about whether the jury should be played the recording. Foulkes, another expert, said 'I wouldn't have thought it was appropriate to expect a jury to make a decision when the experts can't make that decision' (cited in Innes, 2011, p. 149). The contentious portion was taken out of the tape played to the jury and, in the end, Bain was found not guilty (of course, there was other evidence considered). The point here is that even if an upstanding, honest individual really does hear something being said, this does mean it really was said. The number of linguists consulted in this case and the different possibilities offered for the disputed utterance also makes clear that evidence does not always speak clearly.

Conclusion

While forensic phoneticians cannot establish who said something if they are asked to survey the whole population, as this chapter shows there is a great deal they are able to do. Forensic phoneticians have training and expertise that allows them to make fine distinctions about the way people produce and hear spoken language. The fruits of their research are also crucial in evaluating evidence. From transcribing coughs to resolving unclear recordings, they make valuable contributions to investigations and trials.

8

The pen is mighty

In the previous chapter, linguistic analysis of speech evidence was considered. In this chapter, the focus is on written texts. In the same way that people change their speech in different contexts, they may also change the way they write. And just as there is no such thing as a voice 'fingerprint', there is not a single written style that an individual uses which would make them uniquely identifiable.

The kinds of things that forensic linguists can do with written texts are not dissimilar from the tasks that forensic phoneticians undertake. For example, linguists specialising in text analysis can say something about whether a text has been tampered with. 'Tampering' in this case usually means whether a single individual wrote the whole text, whether it was written under the conditions claimed and whether anything was added later (see Davis, 1994). Linguists may also be able to say something about who wrote a text. Like forensic phoneticians, text analysts can profile writers, and may be asked to assist in identifying the writer of a text.

Some of what can be said about written texts draws on research about how texts are constructed. As Chapter 5 showed, knowing something about the conditions of construction can help identify the features that need particular attention. A feature that appears to indicate guilt may in fact be a sign of innocence. The reverse is also true.

> ## Activity 8.1
>
> Think of a conversation you and another person participated in or were witness to in the last couple of days. It does not need to be anything important, just a conversation that you both think you have a reasonable recollection of. You both need to record accounts of this conversation. Do this separately. First, each person should record themselves telling the story. Afterwards, but not straight afterwards, write down an

account. After you have written it down, listen to the recording. How similar or different is your account from the other person? How similar or different are the written and spoken accounts?

There will probably be a difference between the events you remember and those your friend does; there will probably also be a difference between the spoken account and the written account. It is unlikely that either of you were deliberately misrepresenting your memories; differences between accounts of the most scrupulous of observers can easily arise. In part, this is because people's memories are not as sound as they like to think. Finally, the differences between the spoken and written versions may be related to the mode of production. A written transcription of a spoken text is very different from a text that has been written down to start with. Paying attention to these differences can help to understand how a text came into being and, thus, how it needs to be understood. I will refer back to this activity throughout the chapter.

Put it in writing

If a person confesses to a crime, there is usually a signed statement to that effect (see Chapter 5). But what happens if the suspect later claims that the confession was fabricated or forced? Such miscarriages of justice are well documented (Coulthard, 1996; Gudjonsson, 2002) and the number of people confessing to crimes they did not commit is higher than people imagine (Gudjonsson and Pearse, 2011). Telling the difference between an authentic and fabricated statement is not always easy; but it is important.

In many jurisdictions, the signed statement is supposed to be written in the suspect's own words. However, as has been shown (Chapter 5), the statement may be elicited through question and answer and written down by one of the police officers conducting the interview. There may be no obvious indication that the statement is actually the result of an interview, quite the reverse, as the individual signs the statement and it is written in the first person. Further, the label 'statement' suggests that it is a transcribed monologue, elicited and written down in one session without interruption and in the suspect's own words. If the statement is thought to have a single author, it will be read and understood accordingly.

The trouble with 'the'

Paying attention to a text's production is important. To make this clear, the confession of Derek Bentley will be examined. This is a well-known case, and it has been extensively analysed by linguists (Coulthard 1994a, 2002, 2006; Olsson, 1997).

In 1952, Derek Bentley was out with his friend Chris Craig. They had planned to commit a robbery, and after two sites were found to be unsuitable because of people being present nearby, they decided to break into a warehouse. They were seen, and the witness called the police. The police promptly arrived and surrounded the building. Bentley gave himself up but Craig had not yet been detained. Craig shot a police officer who later died. At the time, murder was a capital offence in the United Kingdom. Craig, being a minor, could not be sentenced to death but Bentley could. For him to be charged with murder, it had to be shown that he knew Craig had a gun and that using the weapon was, at least, foreseeable.

The following is the statement used at trial. The sentences have been numbered so they can be referred to later.

Activity 8.2

Read the statement bearing in mind what has already been said about the construction of statements. What would the prosecution have relied on? Given the previous activities, is there anything that seems odd? Did Bentley know that Craig was carrying a weapon?

(1) I have known Craig since I went to school. (2) We were stopped by our parents going out together, but we still continued going out with each other – I mean we have not gone out together until tonight. (3) I was watching television tonight (2 November 1952) and between 8 p.m. and 9 p.m. Craig called for me. (4) My mother answered the door and I heard her say that I was out. (5) I had been out earlier to the pictures and got home just after 7 p.m. (6) A little later Norman Parsley and Frank Fazey called. (7) I did not answer the door or speak to them. (8) My mother told me that they had called and I then ran out after them. (9) I walked up the road with them to the paper shop where I saw Craig standing. (10) We all talked together and then Norman Parsley and Frank Fazey left. (11) Chris Craig and I then caught a bus to Croydon. (12) We got off at West Croydon and then

walked down the road where the toilets are – I think it is Tamworth Road.

(13) When we came to the place where you found me, Chris looked in the window. (14) There was a little iron gate at the side. (15) Chris then jumped over and I followed. (16) Chris then climbed up the drainpipe to the roof and I followed. (17) Up to then Chris had not said anything. (18) We both got out on to the flat roof at the top. (19) Then someone in a garden on the opposite side shone a torch up towards us. (20) Chris said: 'It's a copper, hide behind here.' (21) We hid behind a shelter arrangement on the roof. (22) We were there waiting for about ten minutes. (23) I did not know he was going to use the gun. (24) A plain clothes man climbed up the drainpipe and on to the roof. (25) The man said: 'I am a police officer – the place is surrounded.' (26) He caught hold of me and as we walked away Chris fired. (27) There was nobody else there at the time. (28) The policeman and I then went round a corner by a door. (29) A little later the door opened and a policeman in uniform came out. (30) Chris fired again then and this policeman fell down. (31) I could see that he was hurt as a lot of blood came from his forehead just above his nose. (32) The policeman dragged him round the corner behind the brickwork entrance to the door. (33) I remember I shouted something but I forgot what it was. (34) I could not see Chris when I shouted to him – he was behind a wall. (35) I heard some more policemen behind the door and the policeman with me said: 'I don't think he has many more bullets left.' (36) Chris shouted 'Oh yes I have' and he fired again. (37) I think I heard him fire three times altogether. (38) The policeman then pushed me down the stairs and I did not see any more. (39) I knew we were going to break into the place. (40) I did not know what we were going to get – just anything that was going. (41) I did not have a gun and I did not know Chris had one until he shot. (42) I now know that the policeman in uniform that was shot is dead. (43) I should have mentioned that after the plain clothes policeman got up the drainpipe and arrested me, another policeman in uniform followed and I heard someone call him 'Mac'. (44) He was with us when the other policeman was killed. (Coulthard, 2006, p. 4)

The prosecution focussed on two of the sentences in the statement:

(23) I did not know he was going to use the gun.
(41) I did not have a gun and I did not know Chris had one until he shot.

The use of the definite article in (23) '*the* gun' suggests that the gun is 'given' information. Thus, the inclusion of 'the gun' in this statement was used to argue that Bentley did know that his friend had a gun. Further, the use of the indefinite article in (41), long after the use of the definite article, was used to argue that Bentley was being deceptive in his statement as once something is treated as given it would normally continue to be treated in this way. If it is accepted that the statement was taken as a dictated monologue, in Bentley's own words, it seems reasonable to say that Bentley knew his friend had a gun. However, there are features in the confession that suggest another scenario.

The first feature, the use of 'then', might not seem unusual, even though it is used ten times in a statement of under 600 words (Coulthard, 1994a, p. 32). What is unusual is its syntactic position; it is used post-positionally, that is, it occurs after the subject of the sentence.

(11) Chris Craig and I **then** caught a bus to Croydon.
(15) Chris **then** jumped over and I followed.
(16) Chris **then** climbed up the drainpipe to the roof and I followed.

Examination of corpora (collections of language) shows that this position is unusual (Coulthard, 1994a, p. 32). Moreover, this particular placement has been found to be a common feature of police language (Coulthard, 1994a, p. 33; Fox, 1993). In short, post-positioned 'then' is not common in 'normal' speech. More significantly, in Bentley's oral testimony there were only two instances of 'then' and neither occurred in this position.

The second feature is a textual one and relates to negative clauses (Coulthard, 2006). In Activity 8.1 above, how many negative statements were there? When constructing a narrative people tend to recount what did happen rather than what did not happen. Further, clauses and sentences in a text tend to be ordered according to 'sequence relations' or 'matching relations' (Winter, 1974, cited in Hoey, 2001, p. 30). Sequence relations in a narrative are usually temporal. That is, people recount first what happened first, then they report what happened next and so on. A cause and effect relation is also a kind of sequence relation; a particular kind of temporal relationship. Matching relations are less common in a narrative. These include contrasts, similarities and a general statement followed by an example. Such relations are more common in texts making an argument. The point is that texts are structured. Clauses relate to each other.

Bearing in mind those two points – that people tend to report what did happen and that narratives make use of sequence relations – it is worth looking at some of the negative clauses in Bentley's statement.

> (16) Chris then climbed up the drainpipe to the roof and I followed. **(17) Up to then Chris had not said anything.** (18) We both got out on to the flat roof at the top.
>
> (22) We were there waiting for about ten minutes. **(23) I did not know he was going to use the gun.** (24) A plain clothes man climbed up the drainpipe and on to the roof.

The placement of the negative statements is odd. There is nothing in sentence (16) or (18) that mentions talking. Likewise, there is nothing in sentence (22) or (24) that alludes to Chris or the gun. It is very difficult to infer any relation between the negative sentence and those on either side of it. However, if these negative sentences are removed, there is a straightforward sequence relation between (16) and (18) and between (22) and (24).

Without any other reasonable explanation of the statement's 'odd' features, it is easy to think that these features are indicative of guilt. This seems to have been the view at the original trial. In summing-up the evidence for the jury, the trial judge said:

> Then in his statement he said: 'I didn't know he was going to use the gun'. Again, if he said that, it shows that he knew it. ... Then later in his statement he said he did not know 'Chris' had a gun till he shot. That, of course, is quite inconsistent with what he said earlier in his statement. You can have the statement when you go to your room, if you like. He did say 'I didn't know he was going to use the gun', and then he said afterwards 'I didn't know Chris had one until he shot'. (*R* v *Derek William Bentley* (Deceased) [1998] EWCA Crim 2516)

The original trial judge urged the jury to use their common sense when coming to a verdict, describing this is as the 'great virtue of trial by jury' (136F). Common sense is necessary in jury deliberations as elsewhere. But what common sense would say about the statement if one accepts that it was dictated is different to what common sense would say if it was known to be produced in some other way.

If the statement was taken by interview, it is easy to see how 'the gun' entered the narrative.

Police: Did you know he was going to use the gun?
Bentley: No

Research about what occurs in statement taking sessions (Chapter 5) suggests what happened next. The question would be reformulated as a negative statement – 'I did not know he was going to use the gun' – and recorded in writing. Common sense may then suggest that the oddities in the statement are well explained by the statement having been taken through question and answer. It should be noted that at the time of Bentley's case it was possible to elicit verbal evidence by interview or statement (either written or dictated). However, if an interview took place, all questions and answers were to be recorded longhand (Coulthard, 2006). The police testified that the statement had been dictated; Bentley claimed that at least some of it had been produced as a result of questioning.

In 1998, the case was heard by the Court of Appeal on the recommendation of the Criminal Cases Review Commission. In its judgment, the court noted that it was now impossible to know exactly how the statement was taken. However, the court also admitted the possibility that the incriminating sentence was 'in fact no more than the officer's record of the appellant's negative answer to the question "Did you know he was going to use the gun?"' (pgh 123). The evidence that led to this finding included material from linguists. This example shows that linguists are sometimes necessary to help common sense along the right path.

Do you really remember?

Before leaving statements and witness accounts, there are some other common sense ideas that need to be discarded. In the texts produced for Activity 8.1, were the recollections of the words spoken the same for both people? Such convergence is highly unusual. While people might think they can remember exactly what someone else has said, research shows that people are much better at retaining the 'gist' of utterances

(Campos and Alonso-Quecuty, 2006; Coulthard, 1994b, p. 420). That is, rather than recalling verbatim what someone has said, people tend to recall the message the person was trying to convey. Indeed, if accounts are too similar, it can be a sign, if not of falsification, then perhaps of manipulation (Tyrwhitt-Drake, 2003).

People also tend to think that their memories of events are reliable, especially if they have witnessed an accident or a crime. After all, common sense would say that people know what they saw. It turns out that what people remember depends very much on the questions asked. In a now classic set of experiments, Loftus tested the effect of word choice in questions seeking information from witnesses (1975, 1996). In one case, subjects were shown footage of a car accident in which there was, in fact, no broken headlight. Some respondents were asked 'Did you see *the* broken headlight', while others were asked 'Did you see *a* broken headlight'. Affirmative answers were higher when the definite article was used.

Likewise, estimations of how fast the vehicles were travelling were influenced by verb choice.

1. About how fast were the cars going when they smashed into each other?
2. About how fast were the cars going when then collided with each other?
3. About how fast were the cars going when they bumped each other? (Loftus, 1975, p. 562)

The use of 'smashed', as in (1), received higher estimates of speed than the other two choices. Even in relation to the most straightforward facts, what a person remembers depends on what she is asked.

This research suggests that attention needs to be paid to the way in which texts, especially legal texts in a trial, are produced. In the Bentley case, one of the main reasons for analysing the statement was to consider which mode of production best explains its features. It also makes clear that 'common sense' is not always what it seems to be; for 'common sense' to come to the right conclusion, the right information needs to be available.

- The way a text is constructed is relevant to its interpretation.
- Common sense is not always enough for the appropriate interpretation of texts.

‛ticular hand?

As with the previous chapter, it is not possible to say definitively that a particular person wrote a particular text if the possible writer could be anyone at all. Just as people do not have voice fingerprints, neither do they have written fingerprints. Theoretically, individual idiolects exist, but this does not mean that author identification is straightforward (Coulthard, 2004). Usually, a linguist will be asked to determine who, from among a limited set of authors, wrote a text. Examples of writing from all possible authors will need to be available. These are then analysed before attention moves to the 'suspect' piece of writing (Grant, 2013).

Idiosyncratic features have been useful in some cases. The so-called Unabomber case in the USA shows this in relation to written material (Coulthard, 2006). The bomber sent a manifesto to newspapers demanding it be published in return for stopping the protracted bombing campaign. When published, a man contacted the police saying that the document's use of the phrase 'cool headed logician' sounded like his brother. The brother was arrested and when his residence was searched, other documents were found which strongly suggested he was the bomber. Terms in the manifesto that were found to be distinctive were:

> at any rate; clearly; gotten; in practice; moreover; more or less; on the other hand; presumably; propaganda; thereabouts; and words derived from the roots argu* and propos* (Coulthard, 2006, p. 3).

These findings were challenged on the basis that these words are neither unusual nor distinctive. However, analysts searched the internet and found that the only documents which contained all these terms were in fact versions or extracts of the manifesto. Note that in this case a great deal of writing was available which was directly related to the suspect text. Moreover, the suspect was identified by his brother.

While not all authorship identification cases are the same, the process the linguist follows is similar. There are a number of variables that need to be considered when approaching a written text. The first is the context. An email to a friend is very different to one applying for a job. Some features may stay the same, but there may also be some that change simply because of the kind of email being written. Second, linguists do not look for a single unique identifier, rather a number of features will be examined and attention paid to their rate of use (Eagleson, 1994, p. 363–4; Grant, 2013). This means that a great deal of work in this area uses statistical methods which are becoming more and more sophisticated all the time. Indeed, academics have worked on models that allow us to say something about the reliability of attributions employing statistical methods (Chaski, 2001; Grant, 2007). These models help in addressing the standards of the courts in relation to expert evidence. In particular, courts in the US routinely require that the Daubert criteria are satisfied, that is, that: (1) the theory has been tested; (2) it has been peer reviewed; (3) it is generally accepted; and (4) whether there is a known error rate (Grant, 2007, p. 2; see also Solan and Tiersma, 2004). I will not deal with the statistical models or the rules of evidence here. Rather, I will consider the kinds of features that linguists look for when dealing with one specific genre.

Keeping it short

The text message (SMS) is a relatively recent communication technology. Fortunately, changes in technology can be dealt with by linguists. Indeed, the variation possible in new forms, like text messaging, may be an advantage for linguistic analysis.

Activity 8.3

With some of your friends and family, gather together some texts (SMS) that you have sent and received. Try to get a few from the same author. Write them out exactly as they were received. What kind of differences are there between texts? Do people have a consistent text style?

If the people in your texting network are diverse enough, you may have found features such as using letters to stand for syllables (l8er; b4), numbers for words (2), abbreviations and acronyms (lol; ttfn) (Thurlow, 2003). Because texting has features of both written and spoken language, words may be written to represent a spoken style, 'ave' for 'have' or 'gonna' for 'going to', for example. And while people do not always text in exactly the same way, there are some features that may be demonstrably habitual. For this to be shown, a body of texts from the same person are needed. Remember that habits are not rules, so there may not be complete consistency in an individual's texts. Moreover, context needs to be considered; a text to a relative may look a bit different from one sent to a close friend.

McMenamin (2010) puts forward three models that we can use to think about this kind of analysis. While he is not dealing specifically with text messages, the general models are nevertheless relevant. The first is the resemblance model – which involves trying to ascertain whether a particular person, from a small range of people, may have written a text (McMenamin, 2010, p. 490). The second is the consistency model; this asks whether the features of the texts are consistent or not. This is often used to figure out if a set of texts may have been written by the same person. McMenamin points out that this may be the first step in a resemblance model task (2010, p. 490). The final model is the population model, where there is a large pool of possible authors (2010, p. 490). The task here may be much more like speaker profiling (see Chapter 7) in that a linguist may only be able to provide some general pointers in relation to the writer. For example, the linguist may be lucky enough to find a particular lexeme that is part of a regional dialect. Likewise, given that some people use an 'eye dialect' when they text, some information about the texter's pronunciation may be hypothesised. I now consider a particular case in which linguists examined text messages.

Missing

In 2005, Jenny Nicholl went missing. Her parents received text messages from Jenny's phone. While the text messages claimed that Jenny was fine, the police were not sure that Jenny had actually sent the texts, and so asked linguists to examine the texts (Amos, 2008; Grant, 2010; Olsson, 2009). The linguists had access to a number of text messages and examined them to look for similarities and differences.

Activity 8.4

Consider the following texts. Were they written by the same person?

1. u have booked2go to London2day?
2. im hopin2ave it 2morrow
3. i am goin2 yr place
4. ya make it 2 London?

These texts draw on some of the variations that the linguists looking at the material found. Of course, they had more texts to work with and there was also some variation in text length (Olsson, 2009, p. 60). The texts sent after Jenny went missing said that she was starting a new life and did not want to be found. Note that stress, big life changes or even a new phone may change the way people use texting language (Olsson, 2009, p. 61). Nevertheless, there were some differences, and the details allowed the linguists to conclude that there did seem to be a change in style. While (1) has 'u' for 'you', text (4) used 'ya'. While (2) expressed 'I am' as 'im', text (3) uses 'i am'. The use of spaces in later texts was also thought to be noteworthy. While Jenny appeared to have a habit of putting words together with a number in the middle ('booked2go'), later texts inserted one or more spaces around the numbers. Texts known to be from the main suspect had spaces like this. This was used to argue that he, rather than Jenny, sent the later texts.

As both Olsson and Coulthard note, the linguists treated the evidence with 'some caution' (Amos, 2008; Olsson, 2009, p. 61). However, when the case came to trial, evidence about the movements of the accused was presented along with information about where the texts were sent from (Amos, 2008). The accused had hired a car, and the mileage was consistent with a narrative that saw him sending the texts from the places indicated by mobile phone records. Amos (2008) writes, 'The prosecution told the jury this all had to be more than just an unhappy coincidence for the defendant. They agreed and unanimously found him guilty of killing Jenny'.

- Paying attention to small details is important for forensic text analysis.
- While we do not have linguistic fingerprints, we do have habits.
- Text analysis is often used in conjunction with other evidence in particular cases.

• Forensic linguists are cautious in expressing any absolute certainty about authorship of texts.

Lying? Can we tell?

'Obviously, the linguist has no way of evaluating the truth of what was said *in* a text but fortunately can, at times, evaluate the truth claims made *about* a text' (Coulthard, 1994b, p. 415). In Chapter 4, it became clear that lying can be very difficult to detect. It was noted that lying (violations of the maxim of quality) may well be uncovered because of other evidence. It is not usually possible to know, just by looking at a text, whether it was truthful or not. It is, however, often possible to say something about how a text was constructed.

Clearly it would be terribly useful for law enforcement professionals to be able to detect lies (Lacerda, 2009). No doubt their experience of crime and crime narratives will mean they develop some 'instincts' about whether someone is telling the truth. But this may be based on past experience and is perhaps more properly described as being about plausibility than truth. Even so, a narrative can be true even if it seems highly implausible. It has been suggested that some 'truth wizards' do exist, that is, people who are highly skilled in detecting lies (O'Sullivan, 2007). For people who are not wizards, the value of having some way of determining what might be a lie is obvious, and it is something that researchers have considered.

Activity 8.5

Assuming the narratives you told in Activity 8.1 are true, now write a short account of something that did not happen. Do not look at your other narrative; just make something up. When you have made it up, compare it to the 'real' narratives from before. Are there differences?

The research in this area concludes that, while there is no sure sign that something is a lie, there are some features that suggest further investigation may be needed. Some of these features may have been present in the narrative produced for Activity 8.5, but whether they are present depends on a few things. It may be that a made-up story is based on something that actually happened, that is, the story was not completely made up. In such a case, the 'tell-tale' features may not appear. The presence of significant features may also depend on the imaginative skill of the writer.

Researchers in the FBI conducted a study which looked at written statements (Adams and Jarvis, 2006). They paid attention to six features which, based on other work, they thought might be helpful in indicating the truth of a narrative. These were: equivocation, including hedges and qualifiers; negation; textual structure, specifically, the prologue, incident and epilogue; inclusion of sensory detail; information about emotional state; and using quoted discourse.

In this research, it was possible to find out which statements were most likely to be true and which were not by choosing only cases with clear outcomes (Adams and Jarvis, 2006, p. 10). The statements had to be connected with 'conviction, overwhelming case evidence, or corroborated confession' (2006, p. 10). It should also be noted that these statements were written by the witness/suspect. As shown above, this is significant. And while the researchers did not find a fool-proof method for detecting deception, they did uncover some indicators. Truthful accounts tended to include sensory detail when recounting the criminal incident, while deceptive ones did not (2006, pp. 15–16). Thus, deceptive accounts may have included sensory details in the prologue but not anywhere else (2006, p. 16). Emotions tended to be included in the epilogue of the true statements (2006, p. 16). And as one might expect, there was some correlation between deception and the use of equivocation and negation.

Because of the kinds of features involved, however, caution is required. The methods are not 'ends in themselves but are instead the means for gaining a full account from victims and suspects' (Adams and Jarvis, 2006, p. 20). The features have to be interpreted in light of other details and context. For example, a witness standing 200 metres away from a criminal event might report 'I heard a car starting up, a very loud car so probably a big one. I couldn't see it, but I could hear it well enough'. Even though there is negation and equivocation, to express certainty here would probably be rather suspicious. Thus, while it would be nice to all be truth wizards, analysis of texts alone is not going to be enough to make final judgements about whether or not someone is lying.

• When looking at texts, attention has to be paid to their conditions of production and to as many features as possible.

- There may be more than one explanation for the features that are found.
- Linguistic detail can be useful in directing investigations as well as finally trying cases.

Conclusion

Forensic linguists can be called on not only to analyse texts for the purposes of a trial, they may also be called to help in the early stages of an investigation. Common sense sometimes needs to be supplemented by other information in order to reach the most appropriate conclusion. And, while it is not usually possible to be absolutely certain, it is possible for linguists to say something about written texts and their authors. Under the right conditions, they may even be able to point to the most likely writer. The small details of texts are crucial in these cases.

9

Once upon a time

'Narrative is a central function of language' (LeGuin, 1992, p. 39). People tell stories all the time and while it is tempting to think of a 'story' as either a distracting entertainment or a piece of art, narratives are present in the most unexpected of places. In this chapter, the focus is on narratives in a legal frame. Thus, it connects to topics covered previously, including courtroom language and witness statements (Chapter 5). Narratives occur in trials, judicial instructions to the jury and in the decisions which judges make in civil cases. Finally, narratives are also told about trials, and are an important way of making sense of the law. Narrative is a central function of language in a legal context.

It's not what you say …

While narratives differ widely, it is possible to talk about narrative structure. This structure can be found simply by dividing a narrative into small parts, analogous to, but generally larger than, the parts of a sentence. Usually, a narrative is divided into clauses, each having one main past tense verb. Once the narrative has been divided in this way, it can be analysed in terms of the syntagmatic and paradigmatic axes (Chapter 2). Taking this approach makes clear that all narratives are the result of choices; about what is included and what is left out, and how the events are ordered. It is important to remember that narratives can only ever be versions of reality; they are more or less representative of what really happened; more or less plausible and more or less satisfying.

Lawyers understand the significance of the choices narrative allows. While the things included (and omitted) and their ordering is clearly important, there are also choices that can be made about how events, people and places are described. Because narratives are representations of reality, the choices made in a narrative can have profound effects on the way the jury understands the 'facts'. For example, in the O.J. Simpson trial, there was discussion in court, without the jury present, about the labelling of one of the pieces of evidence.

Example 9.1

Mr. Cochran: I'm talking about the label of this evidence, and I just think it's inappropriate to call it a blood trail. So I am asking the court – when I saw this last night, we weren't on the record or whatever. So now is the time. She hadn't put it out. Now is the time. I'm just saying we should – if she wants to call it blood at Bundy, I have no objection. I object to the use of the word 'trail' (The Simpson Trial Transcripts, February 9th 1995 http://walraven.org/simpson/feb09.html).

Counsel for the prosecution argued that the word 'trail' is simply 'descriptive'; that it is a fact. The defence lawyer, Mr Cochran, did not agree: 'five drops of blood. That does not make a trail among most reasonable experts'. The point is not about expertise, but about what the word 'trail' suggests; something substantial and directional. This example makes clear that the use of one word instead of another can have persuasive effects (Cotterill, 2004). In short, 'Choice of words expresses an ideological position' (Stubbs, 1996, p. 107) and ideologies carry with them beliefs and values. This means that the careful selection of a word can invoke a whole argument and point of view (see Danet, 1980).

   Cotterill (2004) explains how word choice can be crucial to the creation of an appropriate 'lexical landscape'. She examines data to show that in the questioning of witnesses, the difference between 'friend' and 'acquaintance' or 'hit in the face' and 'smash in the face' can have an effect on how a narrative is understood. Taking all these lexical choices together, it is possible to talk about a 'lexical landscape' constructed by a lawyer that both frames the witness's testimony and has persuasive effects. The ways in which the 'who', 'where' and 'what' are encoded do more than just recount a series of events. These choices also help make an argument, persuade a jury or suggest that the events the witness describes never actually happened.

Activity 9.1

Brenda Danet (1980) examined the lexical choices made in a trial where a doctor was being tried for manslaughter because of a late-stage abortion he performed. What kinds of lexical choices might the prosecution and defence make in such a case?

The choice of one word over another can have significant effects in a narrative. For these to have their full effect, the narrative needs to be well structured, so that the events recounted make sense in relation to each other. While it is possible to simply apply the syntagmatic and paradigmatic axes to narrative, there are other ways of describing narrative structure. William Labov (1972) developed a very useful model for analysing narratives that is widely used. He gathered oral narratives from young men in inner-city New York and found that these kinds of narrative monologues often have a five part structure:

1. Abstract – this describes what the story is about. It may only be a short section, but it sets the scene and in many cases, primes expectations.
2. Orientation – the orientation section provides information about the time, the location and the people involved. It describes the 'where', 'when' and 'who' of the narrative.
3. Complicating action – this is the main event. While 'complicating action' may suggest that something else has happened before, it is the event that the narrative focuses on.
4. Evaluation – the evaluation is an assessment of the events, whether they were positive, funny or tragic.
5. Resolution – this is what happened in the end, how the story 'turned out'.
6. Coda – this final section bridges the gap between the story and the communicative context in which it takes place. In a conversation, it brings the participants out of the story world and back to the immediate interaction.

These are the parts of 'fully formed' narrative but they are not all obligatory. A 'minimal narrative' may simply have two past tense clauses ordered in relation to each other. For example, 'he went out; he came back' is a minimal narrative in that it communicates two events in a temporal relation. This becomes clear if the order is reversed; 'he came back; he went out' tells a different story. It is also important to note that Labov's sections may not be completely self-contained. In particular, the evaluation may be spread throughout the narrative (Labov, 1972, pp. 369–70).

In order to ascertain what a narrative is doing, and whether the choices made are appropriate, attention needs to be paid not only to the narrative structure but also to the context in which the narrative takes place. In an everyday situation, a narrative has to be tellable; there has to be a point. Labov notes that 'Pointless stories are met (in English) with the withering rejoinder, "So what?"' (1972, p. 366). This is also true in a legal context in so far as narratives have to have a point. The point of a courtroom narrative, however, will relate to the argument the lawyer is making. In the courtroom, a narrative also has to be plausible if it is going to have any persuasive effects. There is another important difference in the courtroom situation; the narrative will not be told by a single speaker. Rather, the narrative has to be constructed through the routine of question and answer.

- Narratives have a structure.
- Narratives can be analysed in terms of:
  - what is included and what is not;
  - the ordering of events;
  - the detail of representation.

Narratives in pieces

Given that witnesses have limited speaking rights in a courtroom (see Chapter 5), whether a narrative is told, and how it is told, depends very much on the lawyer's questions. Because of this, Harris (2001) proposes that a modified Labovian structure is more suitable for analysing narratives from witnesses. The modified structure includes the 'orientation', the 'core narrative' (which more or less corresponds to the complicating action), any 'elaboration' which may be present and the 'point' of the narrative (Harris, 2001). The point is like the evaluation, but concerns the relevance of the narrative to the case being tried. As such, it is 'addressed explicitly to the jury' (Harris, 2001, p. 60). It is labelled in this way as the affective stance of the witness (whether

they found the events happy, tragic or humorous) may be less important than establishing a fact or detail that is relevant to the case being
tried and the argument the lawyer is trying to make. Likewise, elaboration is important in the courtroom as it 'provides further details, clarification, explication etc of the core narrative' (Harris, 2001, p. 60). The
details provided by the witness may well be the most important contribution a witness can make. There are two reasons for this. First, the
narratives told in court will be assessed in relation to the details
of narratives from other witnesses as well as in relation to other available evidence. Second, the details provided by a witness can help
assess whether their narrative is credible.

Activity 9.2

The following is an extract from the O.J. Simpson criminal trial. Try to
identify the narrative here. It might help to imagine that there is only one
speaker. Use Harris's modified Labovian structure to describe the structure. What differences are there from a 'normal' narrative? The witness
(A) is Robert Riske, the first police officer called to the scene. The lawyer
(Q), the head prosecutor Ms Clarke, has called this witness.

1. Q: At approximately 12:09 a.m. Did you receive a call directing you
   to that general location?
2. A: To 874 South Bundy, yes.
3. Q: What was the nature of the call that sent you to 874 South Bundy?
4. A: It came out as a burglary suspect and the statements of the call
   said it was unknown person knocking on the victim's door.
5. Q: And ringing the doorbell?
6. A: Yes, ma'am.
7. Q: And in response to that particular call did you go to the location?
8. A: Yes.
9. Q: Tell us what happened.
10. A: As we arrived at the scene we were flagged down by two witnesses
    and a dog. They directed us to 875 and they said there was a dead
    lady on the walkway.
11. Q: Two witnesses? Were they men, women?
12. A: It was a male and a female.
13. Q: And they had a dog with them?
14. A: Yes, ma'am.
15. Q: What did that dog look like?
16. A: It was white and probably two and a half three feet tall.

17. Q: Did they have it on a leash?
18. A: Yes.
19. [many lines omitted]
20. Q: Did you look at the dog?
21. A: Yes.
22. Q: Did you notice anything unusual about it?
23. A: There was blood on his legs and on his paws.
24. Q: Did you notice how far up the legs the blood went on the dog?
25. A: I believe on the rear leg it went up approximately to his knees, just streaks.
26. Q: Streaks of it?
27. A: Yes.
28. Q: All right. What did you do next?
29. A: We went back to the scene, we approached the body of the female, and as we got probably two feet from her body, we discovered the body of a male white laying against the north fence.

(The Simpson Trial Transcripts, February 9th 1995
http://walraven.org/simpson/feb09.html)

In Harris's terms, lines 1–8 constitute the orientation. The core narrative, however, is fragmented; it seems to be present in lines 9–10 and 28–29. Lines 11–18 function as elaboration, asking for details about the witnesses the officer met. Lines 20–26 look like elaboration, however, they also appear to be a precursor to one of the points of the narrative; that the dog belongs to the murder victim. In all these lines, we have only small parts of what could be called core narrative. It is not until line 9 that the lawyer, Ms Clarke, asks the witness to tell her what happened. We then get a short narrative section. At this point, the lawyer asks for elaboration about the witnesses and the dog. A long time after this, the lawyer comes back to the topic of the dog. It is also worth noting that the answers given by the police officer are in very 'objective' language. Harris points out that narrative and more 'objective' factual modes of talk (the 'anti-narrativity mode') exist side by side in the courtroom (Harris, 2004, p. 236). The resulting discourse is thus hybrid in nature (Harris, 2004).

As the direct examination in Activity 9.2 shows, narratives are present in the exchanges between lawyer and witness, even though they are constrained by a number of things. The question and answer format of proceedings, the rules of evidence and whether the lawyer has called the witness will all have an effect on the presence of narrative and its features (Harris, 2004, p. 216). And while the task of the lawyer in direct examination is to construct or elicit a narrative, the cross-examining lawyer basically has two choices. She can construct an alternative narrative or she can undermine the plausibility of the narrative that was given in direct examination (Harris, 2004, pp. 236–7).

Activity 9.3

These lines involve the same witness as above undergoing cross-examination. Are there any narratives here? Mr Cochran, for the defence, is the cross-examining lawyer (Q).

1. Q: And you described for us on many, many, many, many occasions during Miss Clark's direct examination the great pains you took not to walk through this blood or any so-called footprints, right?
2. A: That's correct.
3. Q: And because you knew it was very important to try and preserve the integrity of the evidence; is that correct?
4. A: That's correct.
5. Q: You knew that either the detectives or someone under the direction of the detective, a criminalist, would come out and try to mark these various exhibits; is that correct?
6. A: Right.
7. Q: In fact you also described for us that at some point you saw some blood on the rear gate of the location there?
8. A: Correct.
9. Q: You described for us – remember that?
10. A: Yes.
11. Q: By the way, you never at any time ever saw the photographer taking any pictures of the blood which you claim you saw on that rear gate, did you?
12. A: No, I didn't.
13. Q: Are you aware that the first pictures taken of that blood on June –
14. Ms. Clark: Objection. Assumes facts not in evidence.
15. The court: Sustained, sustained. [This means that the judge agrees with the objection and Mr Cochran has to ask his question in a different way.]
16. Mr. Cochran: Let me phrase it this way, your Honor:
17. Q: Were you aware of whether or not any photographs were ever taken on June 13, 1994, of this blood that was supposedly on that rear gate on that date?
18. A: No, sir.

19. Q: Do you know what date they got back out there to take those photographs?
20. A: No, I don't.
21. Q: If ever?
22. [lines omitted].
23. Q: Were you present at any time any pictures were taken of the supposed blood on the rear gate?
24. A: No.

(The Simpson Trial Transcripts, February 9th 1995
http://walraven.org/simpson/feb09.html)

This is a very different kind questioning to that seen above. By asking the questions in the way that he does, the lawyer reminds the witness and the jury of things the witness had said previously. The point starts developing in line 11, with a question being asked as though it is not particularly important ('by the way'). This leads to a series of questions about what *did not* happen, specifically in relation to the documenting of evidence. In line 11 the lawyer asks whether the witness saw a photographer taking photos of the scenes that the witness has described. This goes on for some time. This is all about point, and the point is made plain in the first lines extracted here. Despite the witness saying repeatedly that certain pieces of evidence were treated carefully, there are a whole series of undocumented absences. The facts here are not disputed, but a narrative consists of more than just facts; it also has a point of view. Here, the lawyer is not so much constructing a narrative as telling the jury how to interpret what they have already heard (Harris, 2004). By pointing out the absences, the events that form the existing narrative can be interpreted differently.

- Narratives provided by witnesses are usually fragmented.
- Narratives may actually be authored by the lawyer.
- Narratives in the courtroom need to have a point.

The instructive narrative

Before the jury are allowed to deliberate, each side will tell an overarching story, one that takes into account all the narratives and details elicited during the process of the trial; these are the closing statements of a trial. In the UK, though not in the USA, the judge then sums up, taking into account the narratives and details produced during the trial by each side in the case. All the details and events about which witnesses have testified are knitted together into a single, albeit complex, narrative which should be unbiased and even-handed (Stubbs, 1996). The jury then needs to decide which narrative is more convincing in the light of the physical evidence and everything they have heard. Because of the adversarial nature of the criminal trial, the jury can thus be understood as the author of the final narrative, which is indicated by their verdict.

At the end of the criminal trial, there is a clear division of labour. In both the UK and the US, the judge will instruct the jury about the relevant law. The jury's task is to establish the facts, and then to apply the law to these facts. To do this, the judicial instruction needs to be accurate and, ideally, comprehensible. A great deal of research has looked at how well juries understand what they are being told by the judge (Charrow and Charrow, 1979; Diamond and Levi, 1996; Elwork, Sales and Alfini, 1982). This body of work indicates that jury comprehension is not always high. This may be because of the way instructions are given.

In the USA, it is not uncommon for a judge to follow 'pattern instructions' (see Dumas, 2000, 2002). These are written texts, sometimes taken from other cases or from legislation (Tiersma, 2001b). As they are written, they will probably lack the features typical of spoken language, and so be difficult to read aloud. But because the directions have been used before, judges may be reluctant to depart from them, as this may lead to their decisions being called into question, appealed against or overruled (on the grounds that the jury had not been properly instructed). As a result, in some cases where jurors have asked for clarification about the law, they have simply been referred back to the pattern instructions (Tiersma, 2001b).

In the United Kingdom, pattern instructions, or specimen directions as they are often called, are no longer encouraged. In the 2010 Bench Book, a kind of handbook for judges about directing juries, the foreword makes clear that 'the objective [is] to move away from the perceived rigidity of specimen directions towards a fresh emphasis on the responsibility of the individual judge, in an individual case, to craft directions appropriate to that case' (Judicial Studies Board, 2010). The Bench Book acknowledges that judges will have developed their own sets of instructions, and it does not prohibit their use, but the clear message is that instructions for juries should be relevant and appropriate to the specific case. The Bench Book retains all the information a judge needs for the directions to be legally accurate. However, rather than being a set of texts that can simply be read out, it now functions more as a guide or checklist.

Bearing in mind what has been said about legal language (Chapter 2), it is worth remembering that explaining the law to non-lawyers is difficult. The judge's task is essentially to 'translate' the language of the law for the lay jury without including elements that should not be there or omitting features which should be (Chapter 6). It seems that the approach of the Bench Book is sound as research on judicial instructions suggests that judicial instruction about the law is better understood when it is conveyed in the 'narrative mode'. This differs from the kind of narrative discussed so far but there are some similarities.

Chris Heffer has conducted a great deal of work on judicial summing up in the United Kingdom (2002, 2005, 2006). His work draws on Bruner's distinction between the narrative mode and the paradigmatic mode (see also Harris, 2004). The narrative mode is 'a way of encoding subjectivity, the nature of human reality, experience, beliefs and emotions ...' (Harris, 2004, p. 218). Thus, it typically refers to the particular, the personal, what has happened, and is concerned with verisimilitude, that is, being true to life (Harris, 2004, p. 218; Heffer, 2003, p. 232). It also tends to be oral in nature, in terms of both form and content. The paradigmatic mode, in contrast, deals with the general and the abstract. It 'is concerned with rationality, the observation and analysis of physical reality, i.e. how things are in the world' (Harris, 2004, p. 218). The paradigmatic mode pays attention to categories, logic, universality, neutrality, what is generalisable and what is true. Thus, it is more like the written mode, and strives to be context free. It is concerned with verifiability rather than verisimilitude (Harris, 2004, p. 218).

Looking at one of the examples that Heffer provides makes the difference between the narrative and paradigmatic mode clear. A British jury is being instructed by a judge about the offence of handling stolen goods. In order to understand what the judge does, it helps to see the definition of the offence in the relevant legislation. Section 22 of the Theft Act 1968 defines the offence as follows:

Example 9.2

22 Handling stolen goods.
(1) A person handles stolen goods if (otherwise than in the course of the stealing) knowing or believing them to be stolen goods he dishonestly receives the goods, or dishonestly undertakes or assists in their retention, removal, disposal or realisation by or for the benefit of another person, or if he arranges to do so.
(2) A person guilty of handling stolen goods shall on conviction on indictment be liable to imprisonment for a term not exceeding fourteen years (Theft Act 1968, s 22).

Activity 9.4

Analyse the language of section 22, paying particular attention to nominalisation and syntactic structure. Think about how best to explain the offence to someone else. It might help to construct a narrative about a particular person to convey the meaning of this section.

There are many features of the paradigmatic mode in this section. This is clear from the syntactic structure and the number of disjunctions ('or'). The main clause is first, 'A person handles stolen goods'. This is followed by a conditional structure ('if') with a very long and complex subordinate clause, which itself contains subordinate clauses. A general individual is referred to, 'a person', and then a list of abstract actions is given. The actions are abstract in that they are not situated in terms of time or place. For someone to be found guilty of this offence, not only must she have done something, she also has to have a particular state of mind; the requirement for both a particular state of mind (*mens rea*) and a particular action (*actus reus*) is routine for criminal offences. Taking all the possible actions and states of mind into account and mapping them out in simple 'true' or 'false' statements would take some time because of all the possible factual scenarios the section is designed to cover.

In explaining the law to the jury, the judge could simply read section 22 and let the jury determine which actions and states of mind are relevant to the case before them. However, as Activity 9.4 shows, understanding this section by analysing the written form is hard enough; having to make sense of it as it is being read out would be harder still. Heffer provides an example taken by a particular part-time judge (called a Recorder in the British system) instructing a jury about this offence.

Example 9.3

Let me just move on then to the offence of handling, because you need to consider the definition of that. This is a bit more complicated and I will go through it rather more slowly with you. (I have to find the right page.) A person handled stolen goods if otherwise than in the course of stealing, knowing or believing them to be stolen, he dishonestly received them. Now, that is the offence which is handling here (cited in Heffer, 2002, p. 241).

This is a slightly shorter version of the original section. The parts left out are those not relevant to the contested facts in the case at hand. As it is really just an extract of the legislation, it has many features of the paradigmatic mode. No reference is made to a particular person or to particular goods. The first two sentences, however, are in the narrative mode. They explicitly comment on what the judge is about to say and include reference to herself ('I') as well as directly addressing the jury ('you'). This is not all that the judge has to say about the offence. (Marks and Spencer is a well-known British department store; the Crown and Robe is a public house.)

Example 9.4

If for example you were standing in Marks and Spencers and you watched a shoplifter steal and then ten minutes later you took the goods from the shoplifter you would receive them knowing that they were stolen. If, on the other hand, you were not in Marks and Spencers when the shoplifter stole that elegant hat and you were outside in the Crown and Robe and somebody came up to you and said, 'Look what I have just nicked from Marks and Spencers', you do not have direct knowledge of it but you have the belief based on what you have been told. So that is the distinction if I can put it that way (Heffer, 2002, p. 241).

In contrast to the first extract from this judge, these lines are largely in the narrative mode; particular examples are used to explain the concept of handling stolen goods. There are some elements of the paradigmatic mode; there is a conditional structure ('If …'.) and a disjunctive ('On the other hand …'). Nevertheless, this is a much better explanation of the offence as it allows the jury to draw on their own experience of the world and their own experience of knowing and coming to know things. The extensive use of the narrative mode means that these lines are less condensed, much less abstract and much easier to process than the original section.

> Simply put, by particularising in this manner, the judge is both showing solidarity with the jurors and making the explanations of law more relevant to their shared everyday experience. This example shows a potentially functional marriage of our cognitive 'odd couple'. The overall structure is paradigmatic, as it must be given the nature of the direction, but the judge tries to breathe back life into the law through careful use of narrativising features (Heffer, 2002, p. 242).

While it may not be possible to avoid the paradigmatic mode altogether, using the narrative mode as much as possible seems to avoid many of the impediments to comprehension that have been identified in relation to jury instructions. While, clearly, the judge needs to be accurate about the law, instructing the jury is also a communicative event and needs to be treated as such (Heffer, 2006).

- Directions about the law should be comprehensible.
- Reliance on written texts may not be conducive to jury comprehension.
- The narrative mode is better suited to instructing juries about the law.

Judgment as story

So far, this chapter has dealt with cases involving a jury. Not all cases are heard in this way, however, and it is worth looking at an example of a judge making a decision. The following example comes from a civil case. Civil law cases 'settle disputes between individuals [and are] not concerned with punishment as such' (Slapper and Kelly, 2004, p. 6). After hearing arguments from both sides, the judge delivers a judgment. The judge's decision needs to be supported by reasons, outlining the application of the law to the facts. Because of this, they can be rather lengthy texts. They often begin by recounting the facts; in this way, they are like judicial summing up in British criminal trials.

Activity 9.5

The following lines are from the opening of a much discussed judgment by the English judge Lord Denning. It sets out the facts of the case. Is it possible to tell what his decision will be? How?

> In summertime, village cricket is the delight of everyone. Nearly every village has its own cricket field where the young men play and the old men watch. In the village of Lintz in County Durham they have their own ground, where they have played these last seventy years. They tend it well. The wicket area is well rolled and mown. The outfield is kept short. It has a good club-house for the players and seats for the onlookers. The village team play there on Saturdays and Sundays. They belong to a league, competing with the neighbouring villages. On other evenings after work they practise while the light lasts. Yet, now after these 70 years a Judge of the High Court has ordered that they must not play there anymore, he has issued an injunction to stop them. He has done it at the instance of a newcomer who is no lover of cricket. This newcomer has built, or has had built for him, a house on the edge of the cricket ground which four years ago was a field where cattle grazed. The animals did not mind the cricket. But now this adjoining field has been turned into a housing estate. The newcomer bought one of the houses on the edge of the cricket ground. No doubt the open space was a selling point. Now he complains that, when a batsman hits a six, the ball has been known to land in his garden or on or near his house. His wife has got so upset about it that they always go out at weekends. They do not go into the garden when cricket is being played. They say that this is intolerable. So they asked the Judge to stop the cricket being played. And the Judge, I am sorry to say, feels that the cricket must be stopped: with the consequences, I suppose, that the Lintz cricket-club will disappear. The cricket ground will be turned to some other use. I expect for more houses or a factory. The young men will turn to other things instead of cricket. The whole village will be much the poorer. And all this because of a newcomer who has just bought a house there next to the cricket ground. (*Miller* v *Jackson* [1977] EWCA Civ 6 (06 April 1977))

In one sense this is a summary of facts, but it is clearly rather more than this (Jackson, 1994). This account creates a particular view of village life, one which is positive and linked with discourses of tradition, community and nature. The 'newcomer' is then introduced. This newcomer is not a welcome addition. While this narrative does communicate what happened, it does so from a particular point of view.

This narrative can be analysed in Labovian terms, but in order to find the point of view from which the narrative is told, it helps to distinguish between the 'narrative plot' and the 'narrative discourse' (Simpson, 2004, p. 20). The narrative plot describes the events as they actually happened and in the order that they happened. The narrative plot is a neutral description of events (in so far as neutral description is ever possible). In contrast, the narrative discourse refers to the particular way in which the narrative plot is conveyed, including the way characters are named, the terms in which events are described and the order in which the events are given. The narrative plot and narrative discourse are not the same. For example, it is not necessary for the narrative discourse to obey the temporal order of the narrative plot.

Activity 9.6

Write out the narrative plot of the story in Activity 9.5. Describe the events in as neutral a way as possible in simple past tense sentences. Compare your account with your colleagues. Then compare them with the original. What differences are there?

There are some important differences between the narrative plot and narrative discourse, though some may have been hard to capture. How to name the 'newcomer' may have been a particular problem. Once this term has been introduced, without an alternative being present in the narrative, it is very difficult to come up with a different label. In contrast, some details are easily disposed of. The narrative plot probably would not provide details about the animals previously living in the adjacent field or their attitude to cricket. The way Denning constructs the narrative discourse is crucial in providing the justification for his decision; that the newcomer cannot stop cricket being played. Rhetorically, if not legally, this decision relies on a particular view of village life in England. This view is communicated through the narrative discourse.

Story in and of the trial

There is one final narrative to deal with. It involves a shift of perspective, in that it involves considering the whole trial from the outside. During a trial or court case, narratives will be told in the courtroom. But the trial itself can become the topic of a narrative. Bernard Jackson (1994) describes both kinds of narratives when he makes a distinction between 'the story in the trial' and 'the story of the trial'. 'The story (told) in the trial' is essentially the story that the jury are evaluating. During a trial, though, and after it finishes, there is another story which is 'the story of the trial'. While the 'story in the trial' involves those people participating in the event (judge, lawyers, witness, jury and so on) the 'story of the trial' is very often constructed and told by those whose only participation is as overhearers. For example, while journalists and members of the public may sit in the court, they are not addressed in the same way as the jury. This does not stop there being communication between the 'trial' and these overhearers. Trials and cases mean something over and above the jury's (or judge's) decision about what happened. What a trial means may become important to people not directly involved. While trials clearly have legal significance, they also have cultural meanings.

Harris (2001) identifies some examples, specifically, stories of the trial constructed by the media. In the case of O.J. Simpson, the story of the trial was as much about racism in America and among police officers as it was about a particular murder. Cotterill (2002) argues that another prominent narrative related to the incompetence of the criminal investigators; this is a story which has relevance beyond the particular case. These representations are connected to the story in the trial, as they are often prompted by the questions asked by lawyers in the courtroom (Harris, 2001, p. 72). Likewise, while lawyers have to deal with the evidence and witnesses in front of them, they too have larger stories in mind, which they may use in trying to persuade a jury. For example, the story about the incompetence of criminal investigators would have been particularly useful for defence lawyers in trials which took place after Simpson. This was such a high profile case that the story would have become well known.

The story of the trial can have effects which endure long after the case ends. Indeed, this story may be the one that is best remembered, even if it is not completely coherent with the story in the trial. Recall that in Chapter 3 a case involving hot coffee was considered. The story of this trial does not accurately represent what happened in the trial. Nevertheless, the story of this trial is used in arguments against the so-called 'litigation explosion', which allegedly involves people bringing lawsuits for entirely frivolous reasons (Meinhold and Neubauer, 2001). There are two things to note: first, it is not clear that there has been a litigation explosion; second, the actual facts of the hot coffee case are probably not widely known. Nevertheless, 'the time when someone sued McDonald's because the coffee was hot' is a story many people 'know' and find plausible. It is a story that fits well with existing stereotypes about law, lawyers and 'pointless' cases (Cole and Dioso-Villa, 2009). The problem is that these stories may influence judgments about other cases and trials, and may even lead to changes in the law (*Hot Coffee*, 2011). Moreover, as juries are drawn from members of the public, these stories may well have effects in the future. While in court a powerful narrative really needs to be coherent with the facts and evidence, the story of the trial is not always constrained in this way.

- There is a story in the trial and a story of the trial.
- The story in the trial can be found in evidence, argument and judgments.
- The story of the trial is often better known than the story in the trial.
- The story of the trial often connects with existing norms, beliefs and ideologies.

Conclusion

Narratives are important in a legal context. They may be fragmented and constrained, but they are, nevertheless, present in the questioning of witnesses, the instruction of juries and the decisions of judges. Moreover, the narratives used in the courtroom do not always stay there. The concept of the story of the trial demonstrates that legal narratives depend on and influence the beliefs and ideas that circulate in the wider world. The story of the trial makes clear the connection the law has with the 'everyday' world.

10

Signs in time and space

In this chapter I consider signs. A number of concepts have already been examined that will be relevant in this chapter, including de Saussure's concept of a sign (Chapter 2), warnings and imperatives (Chapter 3). While linguists have long considered signs in the sense of de Saussure, it is only more recently that signs – in the sense of objects – have attracted attention from linguists. This has happened in the field of forensic linguistics (Mautner, 2012) but also in the context of linguistic landscapes (Jaworski and Thurlow, 2010; Shohamy and Gorter, 2009), multilingualism (Collins and Slembrouck, 2005; Collins, Slembrouck and Baynham, 2011) and geosemiotics (Blommaert and Huang, 2010; Scollon and Scollon, 2003). Researchers in the field of law and semiotics also pay attention to signs and their effects (e.g., Marusek, 2005, 2007; Valverde, 2005; Wagner, 2011).

The approach taken in this chapter aligns best with geosemiotics, which is:

> the study of the social meaning of the material placement of signs in the world. By 'signs' we mean to include any semiotic system including language and discourse. (Scollon and Scollon, 2003, p. 110)

Materiality is the most important thing to notice in this definition; this means the objects of study have a physical presence and thus are located in a particular time and place. Scollon and Scollon include language in their definition. This is helpful as it makes clear that language is also a system of signs. It also suggests that an understanding of how language works can help to examine non-linguistic sign systems. While material signs in the world may or may not include language, they nevertheless communicate meaning.

I begin with some familiar signs in order to introduce the visual and spatial aspects that are important in this area. Because of the materiality of signs, space also needs to be considered. The spatial aspect of signs is analogous to the specific communicative context of utterances. That is, for signs to have a meaning, the producer and receiver have to share communicative codes, whether these are linguistic, pragmatic, spatial or visual.

The first example of signs considered, traffic signs, should make clear the connection between signs and the law. As discussed at the start of this book, the law is always around us. Some of the signs discussed in this chapter clearly show the way in which the law constructs not only space but people. Knowing how to read signs is important when trying to figure out what kind of space is being occupied and who is allowed to occupy it (Doherty et al., 2008).

Heed the octagon!

It is clear that road signs telling drivers to 'stop' or 'give way' have legal origins and effects. If a driver fails to stop at a stop sign, she risks receiving a fine of some kind and, if she does it enough, may even lose her licence. Even for pedestrians such signs can have legal consequences. In some countries, jay walking (crossing without some kind of express indication that this is acceptable) attracts fines. Given that disobeying traffic signals can have negative financial effects, it seems only fair that these signs should be very clear. Naturally, road signs are not primarily about preventing drivers from being fined. They help multiple road users co-exist without harming one another. As a result, signs fall into three categories:

1. Danger warning signs
2. Regulatory signs, and
3. Informative signs (Wagner, 2006, p. 320).

Activity 10.1

This is a very simple task, but that is the point. Draw a stop sign, a give way sign, a sign indicating the speed limit and a warning sign of some kind. Indicate their colour and shape. Was this difficult? Will everyone's pictures be the same?

Road signs are pretty consistent. While travel to new countries may reveal new pictures on warning signs (kangaroos in Australia, for example), an unfamiliar language or orthography, the meaning of the signs will usually be clear. This is the case even though road rules are not the same in different countries; for example, some nations drive on the right rather than the left. While rules about giving way at intersections can be particularly baffling in foreign countries, this is usually because there are no signs to indicate what the rules are.

This consistency is not accidental. It is due (at least in part) to formally agreed rules to be found in the Vienna Convention of 1968, which stipulate a very limited range of semiotic choices for road signs (Table 10.1).

While there is some choice and thus some overlap with respect to the colours available, the shapes permitted are distinctive. The combination of colour and shape is usually enough to discern the meaning of the sign, even if it is completely out of context. That is, a stop sign will be recognised because of its distinctive shape even if it happens to be in the middle of a field. What the sign would mean in such a context may be hard to discern (as noted, signs depend on their physical location for their meaning) but the thing itself is recognisable.

Normally, the physical setting of signs also aids in their interpretation. (This can be compared to the way a speaker's meaning can be

Table 10.1 Road signs in European countries

	Danger warnings signs	Regulatory signs	Informative signs
Sign-perception	To warn and inform road users of a danger	Obligations, restrictions or prohibitions	Travel information (direction, distance, place)
Colour semiotics	Yellow or red	Red or blue	Green or blue
Shape semiotics	Diamond shaped or triangle	Circular, octagonal, triangular inverted	Rectangular, or square

Source: Wagner (2006, p, 321)

grasped because of the context of talk.) For example, an inverted triangle at an intersection probably means 'give way' even if there are no words and even if the normally distinctive colour has been somehow washed away. The key insight here is that for road signs to work, the signs need to be easy to understand and cannot be subject to change (Wagner, 2006, p. 311). The other reason they cannot change is that the association between, for example, red and warnings, is arbitrary. It is a well-known convention, but it is a convention nevertheless.

The way people learn the rules of the road is not unlike the way people learn language and other cultural norms. Consider another space on the road where pedestrians and motorists meet; crossings. At traffic lights, the rules are reasonably straightforward. A green light means go for cars and a green person means that pedestrians can cross. (Though there is some variation in traffic light signalling, especially with respect to how the amber light operates.) Again, this may seem straightforward. But many countries have campaigns exactly to instil semiotic (and behavioural) rules, especially for young children. Whether this takes the form of a song, a rhyme or a helpful character, young children are encouraged to learn the codes of these particular signs and the codes of roadways more generally.

Other rules are learnt through observation. For example, some pedestrian crossings (zebra crossings) are clearly marked. Nevertheless, experience shows that these crossings are not uniformly respected by motorists (or pedestrians), whether out of impatience or simply due to a failure to register the presence of the crossing. For this reason, pedestrians might check to see if oncoming traffic has noted their presence at a crossing, whether the vehicles are slowing down and, thus, whether it is safe to cross. This example indicates that not all signs are equal, even those on the roadside. Even so, most adults appreciate which signs are important. Part of this is through an awareness of the consequences of transgression (speeding will attract a fine; jaywalking may only attract a steely glare) part of it is also through semiotic awareness.

Some signs are more 'legal' than others and it is usually possible to tell the difference. People literate in a set of semiotic codes are able to do this. While 'literacy' commonly describes the ability to read and write, it can be used to describe other competences. (It is worth noting that even written texts rely on familiarity with visual semiotic codes. For example, the difference between printing and cursive script is semiotically relevant in that the choice can be meaningful.) If 'literacy' is used in a broader sense, it is possible to use it to describe all the codes people learn and use when making sense of signs and space. These literacies appear to their owners often as corporeal and automatic; anyone who has crossed a road in a country where cars drive on the 'wrong' side will have experienced this. Finally, literacies can also be exploited for creative effect.

Activity 10.2

It is not always easy to figure out what a sign means. Consider Image 10.1.

Image 10.1 Exploding car

Is it an official sign? What does it mean?

This is in fact a real sign. It means that vehicles carrying explosive material cannot enter the area. This is a sign found in the United Kingdom and in China (and probably other countries too). As it is rather uncommon, people are not always sure about what it means (Foster, 2009). Because this sign is not used a great deal, people do not have the necessary codes to decipher it. People learn to read the signs they see all the time and then treat this ability as 'natural'. Whether we know it or not, we are all literate in a number of semiotic conventions.

- Signs exploit a number of semiotic systems, including language.
- They have meaning only because we know the code that is being used.
- Stable, conventional signs depend on stable conventions.
- Knowing these semiotic conventions is a kind of literacy.

The letters tell a story

Some of the semiotic codes we know are incredibly rich, very common but not usually remarked upon. This is true of fonts and typesetting. The access that we now have to computers and their various standard fonts provides choices that only a few decades ago were only available to a small number of people. Only a generation ago, if someone wanted a particular font she had to either hire a professional with access to the technology and tools to produce them, or learn how to scribe them herself. Now, because of the resources available in this area, all kinds of signs can exploit the communicative potential of fonts (van Leeuwen, 2006). The 'meaning' of the font can interact in various ways with the message content and context. Some examples of a very mundane kind of notice help make this point.

Example 10.1

SMITH ESTATES LTD.
BICYCLES FOUND PARKED AGAINST
OR CHAINED TO THESE RAILINGS
WILL BE REMOVED
WITHOUT FURTHER NOTICE

Example 10.2

𝕭𝖎𝖐𝖊𝖘 𝖜𝖎𝖑𝖑 𝖇𝖊 𝖗𝖊𝖒𝖔𝖛𝖊𝖉

Activity 10.3

Compare and contrast these two examples. Imagine where they might be found. Which one is more likely to be obeyed? Does it make a difference to know that the first is a laminated piece of paper tied to a fence with string and the second is engraved gold lettering on a piece of black slate, screwed into a brick wall?

Both notices state that bicycles will be removed. Thus, they also function as orders conveying the message 'do not leave your bike here'. By highlighting the consequence of not obeying this, the notices are informative and can also be understood as warnings. The use of the modal auxiliary 'will' further strengthens this warning, perhaps even taking it into the territory of a threat. There is no uncertainty here about what will happen to the bikes.

The font in the first example aligns with this clear message. It is a sans serif, block capital font which suggests authority. There is further authority, though of a more specific kind, in that the first line names the owner of the property. The owner is not an individual but a legal entity. This, coupled with the complete deletion of agency from the warning (who will remove the bicycles?), serves to depersonalise the notice. It takes it into the realm of institutional rules. While it may seem obvious, it is also important to note that the sign's meaning depends on the fact that it is attached to railings (Mautner, 2012, p. 198). Not only does its placement lead to the message making sense, it also sends another message: this is private property. This sign works as a boundary marker because of where it is placed (Mautner, 2012, p. 198). If this notice were lying on the street, it is likely to be treated as rubbish rather than any kind of instruction or marker (Mautner, 2012, p. 197).

The other example is rather more compact. However, the choice of font suggests a possible interpretation. If this sign were found near a historic building, the choice of font would make sense. The old fashioned typeface could signal a particular attitude about the surrounding environment. Indeed, some people might be more likely not to leave their bikes near this sign as to do so would 'spoil' the view. The sign itself, with its short message and particular style, invites the reader to consider the aesthetic context of the area and hence not to sully it by leaving a bicycle nearby.

Kress articulates this aspect of signs by paying attention to the materiality of signs, the world and human interaction with them. 'No sign remains, as it were, simply or merely a "mental", "conceptual", a "cognitive" resource. At this point the processes named as affect and cognition coincide absolutely as one bodily effect' (Kress, 2010, p. 77). The sign is in the world and people are in the world with the sign; while the sign depends on abstract systems for its meaning, it also has a tangible reality. Kress argues that signs also communicate something about the sign-maker, about their view of the world. 'As a general principle we can take all signs to be ... an indication of the interest of the sign-maker in their relation to the specific bit of the world that is at issue; an indication of their experience of and interest in the world' (Kress, 2010, p. 77). The materiality of the signs mentioned in the activity can now be appreciated more fully. The laminated piece of paper suggests a particular relationship between the sign-maker and the space. It is not one that seems to have the same level of aesthetic care as the second. 'That sensory, affective and aesthetic dimension is too often ignored and treated as ancillary. In reality, it is indissolubly part of semiosis' (Kress, 2010, p. 78; see also Scollon and Scollon, 2003, p. 16).

- The meaning of fonts and the material of the sign can be relevant to meaning.
- The emplacement of a sign is important as signs construct boundaries and space.
- Signs can tell us about the sign-maker.

Not a normal sign

In Chapter 2, de Saussure's theory of a sign was discussed. But given that many road signs incorporate visual images, it is worth looking at another theory. Charles Saunders Peirce (1977, 1998) makes a distinction between three kinds of signs: icons, indexes and symbol. Peirce's symbol is like de Saussure's conception of the sign. There is only an arbitrary, an unmotivated, connection between the thing that carries the meaning (like a word or sound string) and the meaning it carries. The index, on the other hand, is characterised by some kind of physical connection. The classic example is that smoke is an index of fire; in less technical language, smoke is a sign of fire in so far as (generally) a fire will produce smoke. In this case, there is a causal relationship. For something to be an index there has to be some kind of physical proximity or relationship between the two parts; the connection is not arbitrary but is motivated in some way.

The relationship that constitutes the icon is not completely arbitrary, but nor is it as proximate or motivated as is the case for an index. There is some relationship between the parts, and this is usually some kind of similarity or resemblance. In the case of a road sign warning that children may be playing near a road this can be seen clearly. It is not the case that the physical proximity of the children causes the sign (which would make it an index) but making sense of the picture is not too difficult. This process of comprehension does rely on being familiar with a code, but it is a code less particular than that needed to comprehend something like written language. The code needed to understand icons is a more generalised cultural code. The pictograms on toilets are a good example of this. People know that not all women wear dresses; nevertheless, an outline of a figure with a partly triangular profile indicates 'woman' in many places. This does not need to be explicitly taught, members of a visual culture will simply learn this association. That said, it is easy to take this knowledge for granted. For example, it seems reasonable to say that maps are icons; but constructing and reading maps requires knowledge of all kinds of conventions. That is, not all cultures and people draw maps (or women) in the same way (Anker, 2005).

Activity 10.4

Not all toilets indicate who they are for in the same way. Try and find examples of signs that indicate 'female' and 'male' which do not rely on the human figure described. Restaurants are a good place to look for these.

While linguists describe signs as 'indexing' discourses and ideologies, notice that the indexical relationship is not the same as that between smoke and fire. Rather, this use of 'index' means that a sign points to and also relies on a set of shared conventions around the use of communicative codes (like colours) and what the sign 'stands for' more generally. That is, the term 'index' is used in a metaphorical way, taking for granted the cultural and human construction of semiotic systems.

> All of the signs and symbols take a major part of their meaning from how and where they are placed – at that street corner, at that time in the history of the world. Each of them indexes a larger discourse, whether of public transport regulation or underground drug trafficking. (Scollon and Scollon, 2003, p. 2)

Signs do 'point to' other strata of meaning and human activity. In order to understand signs, especially from a legal point of view, it is important to remember that, while the underlying cultural and human rules may be treated as 'natural', they are in fact ideological.

- Peirce's distinction between the index, icon and symbol complements and extends de Saussure's definition of the sign.
- These semiotic relationships allow us to describe different layers of meaning.

Careful!

Even when warnings are made in writing, visual symbols are often included. On the roadside, for example, it is not always possible to include any written text at all. Other means have to be used to make any danger clear. In such cases, how to avoid the danger is often recoverable from knowledge of what the danger is. Thus, if a sign warns of possible falling rocks, a driver knows to proceed carefully. Sometimes, a (paradigmatic) string of signs is placed on a roadside; a kind of visual sentence. A driver may first be informed that road works are taking place; the next sign might set out a lower than normal speed limit; the following sign may visually indicate that lanes on the road are about to narrow. At the end of the works, signs will inform drivers that the work is over.

Other signs spell out consequences for the disobedient; the warning element is easy to see. On an underground train carriage in London, passengers see the following:

Example 10.3

> £80 penalty fare or prosecution
> if you fail to show on demand a valid ticket for the
> whole of your journey or a validated Oyster card
>
> (Transport for London)

This puts the consequence first even before the rules that need to be followed. The emplacement of this sign is worth considering. Once a passenger sees this particular sign, she will already be on a train. If she has bought a ticket, she is not really an addressee of the sign. If she has not, it is a bit late for her to do much about it. Her only option is to cease riding the train as soon as possible and remedy the situation.

To better understand this notice, it helps to consider the four factors which need to be taken into account when reading signs (Scollon and Scollon, 2003, pp. 10 ff): (1) the social actor; (2) the interaction order; (3) the implied discourse; and (4) place semiotics.

Activity 10.5

Consider these four factors in relation to the sign on the tube. What does this uncover?

The social actor here, the passenger, already has to be on the train to see the sign. Thus, the interaction order includes an institutional voice, in what is clearly an institutional space, telling the passenger that she has to travel with a ticket. The sign itself conveys something else about the interaction order; the author of the sign has the power to impose a fine or even prosecute the disobedient traveller. The implied discourse here is perhaps the most interesting; taking all the other factors into consideration, it would be reasonable to conclude that one of the implied messages is 'fare evaders are criminals'. The discourse of law is clearly signalled by mention of the fine and 'prosecution'. Less legally, there is also an implied message that fare evaders are bad people.

'I am a real sign'

Having looked at the consequences on signs, I now turn to
their preconditions. Mautner
(2012) points out that signs may
explicitly or implicitly refer to
their legal authority. In Example
10.4, the use of 'prosecution'
reminds passengers of the legal
order that the sign indexes. Image
10.2 explicitly names the legislation which authorises its presence and its actions

Image 10.2 Dispersal Area

Unlike signs with an established semiotic code (like road
signs), sometimes signs need to
display evidence of their authority. This can be considered in
terms of felicity conditions
(Chapter 3) in that the message on the sign is not an official speech
act unless it conforms to the conventions stipulated by law. This
may be a legislative requirement, that is, the law may require that
the sign state clearly which law it relies on. Over and above this legal
requirement, signalling the basis of the speech act is also important
for readers of the sign; they need to know how to read it. This is especially true with new, or reasonably rare, signs. In Image 10.2, the
author of the sign is the police and the area it describes has been
created because of power given by the Anti-Social Behaviour Act.
Mautner describes such signs as follows: 'the sign is legally performative – that is, it is an essential element without which the legal
rule concerned cannot be applied in the first place' (2012, p. 199).
This kind of authorising is remarkably common.

Image 10.3 makes it clear that the prohibition against smoking is
not simply an individual or organisational preference; it is against the
law. If the writing was taken off this sign, it would not be clear who the
author was, and the force and importance of the sign may not be quite
so obvious.

Image 10.3 No Smoking

Image 10.4 Designated Public
Place

Activity 10.6

Look at Image 10.4 and identify features discussed so far. Taking them all together, would you say this is a sign, a notice or something else? Note that the sign is actually smaller than the picture suggests; it is approximately A4 size and placed about 6 feet above ground level.

The sign in Image 10.4 designates an area as a 'Designated Public Place'. Its specific meaning is given in written terms, that is, that police 'may require you to' not do something (drink alcohol) or to do something (empty containers containing alcohol). The consequences of not obeying are then spelt out, an exclusion given and a piece of legislation is referenced. This text does a number of things, and it would be reasonable to call it a sign *or* a notice. It signals that the surrounding space is subject to certain rules; but the presence of the text is also necessary in putting these rules into place. That is, a Designated Public Place (DPP) is defined, in part, by the presence of a text which tells you it is a DPP. The text here describes and creates the DPP at the same time. The statement 'This is a Designated Public Place' may look like a declarative, but because of the conventions set out in the Criminal Justice and Police Act (and related Regulations, 2001) it is also a speech act. Thus, this declarative both certifies and announces (a speech act) its own truth value. We are in a self-certifying world of discourse; but it is a world of discourse that has effects in real life.

While all signs structure space, when legal texts are involved, it can be difficult to resist the features, contours and norms of the resulting space (Mautner, 2012). Ignoring a sign does not change the consequences of disobeying it. Mautner notes that signs function as 'boundary markers in both socio-spatial and socio-legal terms, playing an important part in carving up space into public and private areas, and into zones where it is permissible to enact some social roles (e.g., cyclist or angler), but not others (e.g., busker or dog-walker)' (2012, p. 190). Signs construct space, creating areas where some things are allowed and others are not. Further, signs may designate consequences for offending the rules they create. Whether we are consciously aware of it or not, signs do structure and change the spaces in which we move (Mautner, 2012).

- Signs may recite the rules they enforce and the legal regimes that underpin their authority.
- They perform and authorise a speech act at the same time.
- This act may be to create a space, describe its borders or prohibit some activities within the area.
- Legal signs literally construct the spaces in which we live.

Spoken signs

So far, attention has been given to signs and notices which have a physical manifestation. Whether they are official signs on pieces of metal or laminated pieces of paper attached to lampposts, they have a tangible, material presence. There are, however, other kinds of signs: spoken signs. Speech, in terms of conversation and utterances, is composed of signs in the de Saussurean sense, but what I mean by spoken signs here is somewhat different. Spoken signs can, like material signs, be informative, regulatory and indicative of danger, but instead of being written down they are spoken.

The reason I call them signs is that, like material signs, they are situated in space (and time), they have constancy and they structure space. Indeed, they are often simply spoken realisations of something that is written. Another common feature, though it is not essential, is that they are not spoken in real time. That is, these spoken signs are usually recorded messages which are broadcast repeatedly. As they are recorded, each broadcast is exactly the same. Spoken signs have a legal dimension in that their content may set out the law, and their broadcast is only possible if the authors have certain legal rights (property rights, for example). Moreover, they 'relate to what people are allowed to do in a certain place at a certain moment in time' (Mautner, 2012, p. 195).

The examples that follow are all transcriptions of spoken signs heard in train stations and on trains in England. While sometimes train announcements are spoken by a real, live person, these examples are not. They are pre-recorded. In fact, many of them are made up of a number of pre-recorded pieces or chunks. In Example 10.7, the slanted lines are to make clear that the /s/ at the end of 'trains' is pronounced; bold indicates emphasis and (.) indicate small pauses.

Example 10.7

This is a platform alteration (1) the **eighteen fifteen** East Midlands Train/s/ service to (.) Lincoln Central (.) will now depart from platform **3 b**

Example 10.8

This station operates a no smoking policy (.)

Example 10.9

CCTV recording (.) is in operation at this station (.) for the purpose of security and safety management

Example 10.10

This is an important security announcement (.) Please keep your luggage and personal belongings with you at all times (.) Unattended items may be removed and destroyed without warning (.) Please report any suspicious behaviour and unattended items to a member of staff or a police officer (.) Thank you for your assistance.

Example 10.7 is a straightforward informational spoken sign. It makes audible what can be seen on departure boards within a train station. As such, it can be understood as addressing those people who cannot, for whatever reason, see the information displayed on the board. It also reveals its own construction, in that it is clearly put together from separate segments. If you say 'East Midlands Trains service', the /s/ at the end of 'trains' will be deleted, in so far as it will merge with the /s/ in 'service'. In the spoken sign, the /s/ at the end of 'trains' is sounded, indicating a boundary between the chunks that constitute this message. When one knows that 'East Midlands Trains' is the name of a train operating company it is possible to see that this message has been put together from the following chunks:

> [platform alteration declarative] [pause] ['the'] [time hour] [time minute] [train company] ['service to'] [destination] ['will now depart from platform'] [platform number]

This syntax is suitable for any number of companies, destinations, platforms and times. It simply has to be populated with the appropriate pre-recorded parts. As such, it is a very efficient system of spoken signage. It also ensures consistency between informational messages about different trains. This consistency is one of the reasons it makes sense to identify it as a spoken sign.

The other examples are a bit different in that they are regulatory and rely on legal rules for their ultimate authority. While, on the face of it, Example 10.8 looks like an informational sign, if what it is communicating is considered, it is possible to see it as a regulatory sign. It is also a good example of how signs, spoken or not, construct space.

Activity 10.7

Example 10.8 states 'This station operates a no smoking policy'
    Think about the message here. How else could this be communicated? Write all the possibilities down. How do they differ?

In the UK (as in many other countries), smoking is illegal in enclosed public places, including public transport, bus and train stations. This is not what this sign says, however. Rather, it refers to a 'policy'. This spoken sign depends on the same law as Image 10.3. The physical sign that prohibits smoking is pretty consistent around the world. Visual signs need to have the same kind of constancy so that they can be widely and quickly understood (Wagner, 2006). Spoken signs, however, afford some variation because speakers of a language already know the linguistic code. For example, the previous activity may have generated the following:

> You must not smoke in this station.
> Smoking is forbidden in this station.
> Please don't smoke.
> It is illegal for you to smoke here.
> Smokers must be outside the station.

The kind of variation possible can be analysed in detail. First, there might be variation in the subjects and objects identified. In the actual announcement, the people who may want to smoke are not explicitly addressed. There is no reference to 'you' or 'smokers' or anything of that nature. Rather, the subject in the sign is 'this station'. Moreover, because of the reach of the spoken sign, 'this station' covers an area defined in both concrete physical terms (the actual station) and in terms of where the message is audible. Spoken signs are emplaced in a slightly different way to physical signs in that they are heard rather than seen. Just as '*the sign only has meaning because of where it is placed in the world*' (Scollon and Scollon, 2003, p. 29, emphasis in original), for spoken signs, *when* they are placed in the world needs to be considered.

The second variation is how the forbidden action is encoded. In the original message, people are told that there is a 'no smoking policy'. The audience then need to infer from this noun phrase that smoking is not allowed. While this is hardly a difficult conclusion to come to, it is less direct than encoding the activity as a verb, in an imperative, for example, 'Don't smoke here!'. The form of the message suggests that this is an informational smoking sign, telling customers about a policy. But its purpose is really to tell people how to behave in the station. There are two possible reasons for this. The first is that providing information is less face threatening or confronting than telling someone to do (or not do) something. The second reason relates to the specific nature of spoken signs. That is, it is wise to make a spoken sign a bit longer than it absolutely needs to be; it is also advisable to put the important information away from the start of the utterance. Even if a passenger misses the first part of the announcement, she will still hear the part about 'no smoking'. Thus, the rest of this message can be viewed as an audible frame directing attention to the most important part: 'no smoking'.

The final variation that will be discussed has already been mentioned, that is, the directness of the possible variations. This is related to not threatening the audience's face wants. To ask someone to do something or not allow them to do what they want is a face threatening act (Brown and Levinson, 1987). However, the directness of the sign is also related to the construction of space, not just in terms of lines, boundaries, acceptable behaviours and so on, but in terms of mood. Looking at Examples 10.9 and 10.10 will help with this.

Example 10.9, like Example 10.8, starts with a declarative. However, it then provides a reason for what it has just declared. The surveillance is for a positive purpose: 'safety and security management'. The real reason for this spoken sign may be that by law people need to be notified in some way when they are in an area subject to CCTV monitoring. This information may be threatening or reassuring depending on what kind of behaviour a person wants to indulge in. But as the qualifying clause in Example 10.9 frames the CCTV as reassuring rather than intrusive, it can be understood as addressing, and hence constructing, the audience and the space as law abiding and risky respectively.

There is an opening declarative in Example 10.10 too. As mentioned, this seems to be designed to call the attention of the travelling public. The repetition of 'please' and the closing 'thank you' signal politeness. The request that people report suspicious behaviour then involves the audience in the prevention of bad behaviour. Like Example 10.9, this spoken sign warns and informs while addressing and constructing a helpful, law abiding audience. Thus, these spoken signs index a particular relationship between the author of the message and the audience. They position the audience as helpful and courteous but also position them in an unsafe space. Moreover, Example 10.10 indexes a long history of bombs in public places, including train stations, in the United Kingdom.

This chapter started by showing how it is possible to think about visual signs in terms more often used about language. The concept of the spoken sign, however, reverses this relationship. When a vocal warning is given (for example, telling someone to 'watch out!') tone and volume of voice will be used to make the urgency plain. When doing the same in visual terms, other methods need to be used. For example, an exclamation point on a triangular sign is used to express a general warning. The red edging, the triangle and the exclamation point are used to express the same point as the shouting of 'watch out!' Finding a way of capturing in visual form what is usually conveyed vocally (by tone and stress) is called paralinguistic restitution (Thurlow, 2003).

In the case of spoken signs, however, it makes sense to see them as performing a kind of visual restitution. Spoken signs need to use auditory material to communicate what would normally be captured by a written sign. As seen at the start of this chapter, material signs need to be stable, emplaced and quick and easy to comprehend. Semiotic choices, like font, may also project a mood or address the viewer in a particular tone. Spoken signs also need to be stable, emplaced and quick and easy to comprehend. Their stability is managed through the use of recordings of good quality which can be played repeatedly. Emplacement is taken care of by broadcast systems; this is why spoken signs are so common in travel hubs like train stations, bus terminals and airports. The ease of comprehension is managed by constructing spoken signs in such a way that the most important part is rarely first. Finally, the tone or mood is conveyed by exploiting the variation possible in spoken language including the representation of subjects, objects and actions, politeness markers and modality choices.

- Spoken signs translate visual semiotics into spoken conventions.
- They construct space and audiences.
- Like other signs, they rely on communicative conventions and index larger discourses.

Conclusion

In familiar places, people might not pay too much attention to the signs that are placed in the street, on walls or in their places of work. However, signs communicate a great deal about the legal rules that operate and hence how people should behave. Signs do more than simply engage visual attention or tell people how to find a particular place. Signs construct space. Because they are routine and generally well understood, they do not generally attract attention.

> All semiotic systems operate as 'social semiotic' systems ... All semiotic systems operate as systems of social positioning and power relationship both at the level of interpersonal relationships and at the level of struggles for hegemony among social groups ... (Scollon and Scollon, 2003, p. 7).

This deeper message needs to be considered. Signs, and the use that legal regimes make of them, do not just tell people not to do things, they also communicate what kind of person it is acceptable to be. These signs indicate who is an acceptable presence and who is not (Mautner, 2012). Moreover, these signs provide information about how to use a space, as well as authorising others to make sure this happens. Signs do not just construct spaces, they construct people. 'It is just these invisible, almost banal, systems of meaning which form sociopolitical systems that so closely define us and our actions in the world' (Scollon and Scollon, 2003, p. 6).

Coda

A coda brings an audience from the narrative world back to the real world. As I have tried to show in this book, however, the law is very much part of the real world. Legal language, whether written or spoken, depends on the same rules that ordinary language does. The nature of the law means that it adds some of its own conventions of interpretation to texts and communicative interactions. These conventions are not always the same as the ones that linguists or people generally apply and understand. It is this difference that makes paying attention to the language of the law so important.

I hope the material covered in this book has given you a sense of the diversity of the language of law and the utility of linguistic modes of analysis. Work in the field continues at a furious pace providing an ever-increasing literature to draw on and enjoy. I also hope that this book is not the end of your engagement with language and the law, and that you have found at least one of the ideas or examples challenging, fascinating or surprising.

References

Adams, Susan H., and John P. Jarvis. 'Indicators of veracity and deception: an analysis of written statements made to the police.' *International Journal of Speech, Language and the Law* 13(1) (2006): 1–22.

Ainsworth, Janet. '"You have the right to remain silent ..." but only if you ask for it just so: the role of linguistic ideology in American police interrogation law.' *International Journal of Speech, Language and the Law* 15(1) (2008): 1–21.

Ainsworth, Janet. 'A lawyer's perspective: ethical, technical and practical considerations in the use of linguistic expert witnesses.' *International Journal of Speech, Language and the Law* 16(2) (2009): 179–91.

Ainsworth, Janet. 'Curtailing coercion in police interrogation: the failed promise of Miranda v. Arizona.' *Handbook of Forensic Linguistics*. Eds. Malcolm Coulthard and Alison Johnson. Oxford: Routledge, 2010. 111–25.

Amos, Owen. 'The text trap.' *The Northern Echo* 27 Feb. 2008 http://www.thenorthernecho.co.uk/features/leader/2076811.The_text_trap/ accessed 7 August 2013.

Anker, Kirsten. 'The truth in painting: cultural artefacts as proof of native title.' *Law/Text/Culture* 9(1) (2005): 91–124.

ASA. Adjudication on Coty UK Ltd, Coty UK Ltd t/a Rimmel, Complaint Ref: 126569, 2010 http://www.asa.org.uk/Asa-Action/Adjudications/2010/11/Coty-UK-Ltd/TF_ADJ_49421.aspx accessed 7 August 2013.

Atfield, Cameron. 'Appeal over "home brew" conviction succeeds.' *The Canberra Times*, 6 April 2013 http://www.canberratimes.com.au/queensland/appeal-over-home-brew-conviction-succeeds-20130406-2hdz4.html accessed 7 August 2013.

Attardo, Salvatore. 'Violation in conversational maxims and cooperation: the case of jokes.' *Journal of Pragmatics* 19 (1993): 532–58.

Austin, John L. 'Performative Utterances.' *Philosophical Papers*. Oxford: Oxford University Press, 1979.

Austin, John L. *How to do Things with Words*, 2nd edition. Oxford: Oxford University Press, 1980.

BBC News. The Shipman Tapes II 31 January 2000 http://news.bbc.co.uk/1/hi/in_depth/uk/2000/the_shipman_murders/the_shipman_files/613138.stm accessed 22 April 2013.

BBC News. 'Caution on Twitter urged as tourists barred from the US' BBC News Technology 31 January 2012a http://www.bbc.co.uk/news/technology-16810312 accessed 7 August 2013.

BBC News. 'Robin Hood Airport tweet bomb joke man wins case' BBC News Online 27 July 2012b. http://www.bbc.co.uk/news/uk-england-19009344 accessed 7 August 2013.

Berk-Seligson, Susan. 'Interpreting for the police: issues in pre-trial phases of the judicial process.' *Forensic Linguistics* 7(2) (2000): 212–37.

Berk-Seligson, Susan. 'The Miranda warnings and linguistic coercion: the role of footing in the interrogation of a limited-English speaking murder suspect.' *Language In The Legal Process*. Ed. Janet Cotterill. Basingstoke: Palgrave, 2002. 127–45.

Bill of Rights Institute. *Constitution of the United States of America* (1787). http://billofrightsinstitute.org/founding-documents/constitution/ accessed 1 May 2013.

Blommaert, Jan. 'Investigating narrative inequality: African asylum seekers' stories in Belgium.' *Discourse and Society* 12(4) (2001): 413–49.

Blommaert, Jan. 'Language, asylum and the national order.' *Current Anthropology* 50(4) (2009): 415–41.

Blommaert, Jan and April Huang. 'Semiotic and spatial scope: towards a materialist semiotics.' *Working Papers in Urban Language and Literacies, Kings College London*. 62, 2010. http://www.kcl.ac.uk/innovation/groups/ldc/publications/workingpapers/62.pdf accessed 7 August 2013.

Brière, Eugène. 'Limited English speakers and the Miranda rights.' *TESOL Quarterly* 12(3) (1978): 235–45.

Brown, Penelope and Steven C. Levinson. *Politeness: Some Universals in Language Usage*. Cambridge: Cambridge University Press, 1987.

Bucholtz, Mary. 'The politics of transcription.' *Journal of Pragmatics* 32 (2000): 1439–65.

Cain, Kevin G. 'And now, the rest of the story. ... the McDonald's coffee lawsuit.' *The Houston Lawyer,* July/August 2007 http://www.thehoustonlawyer.com/aa_july07/page24.htm accessed 7 August 2013.

Cameron, Deborah. *Verbal Hygiene*. London: Routledge, 1995.

Campos, Laura and Maria L. Alonso-Quecuty. 'Remembering a criminal conversation: beyond eyewitness testimony.' *Memory*, 14(1) (2006): 27–36.

Charrow, Robert P. and Vera R. Charrow. 'Making legal language understandable: a psycholinguistic study of jury instructions.' *Columbia Law Review* 79(7) (1979): 1306–74.

Chaski, Carole. 'Empirical evaluations of language-based author identification techniques.' *Forensic Linguistics* 8(1) (2001): 1–65.

Clarity International. http://www.clarity-international.net/ accessed 7 August 2013.

CNN Politics. 'Obama retakes oath of office after Roberts' mistake.' 21 January 2009 http://articles.cnn.com/2009-01-21/politics/obama.oath_1_oath-president-obama-chief-justice-john-roberts?_s=PM:POLITICS accessed 7 August 2013.

Coldrey, John. 'Aboriginals and the criminal courts.' *Ivory Scales: Black Australia and the Law.* Ed. Kayleen M. Hazelhurst. Sydney: UNSW Press, 1987. 81–92.

Cole, Simon A. and Rachel Dioso-Villa. 'Investigating the "CSI effect" effect: media and litigation crisis in criminal law.' *Stanford Law Review* 61(6) (2009): 1335–74.

Collins, James and Stef Slembrouck (eds.). *Multilingualism and Diasporic Populations: Spatializing Practices, Institutional Processes, and Social Hierarchies.* Special issue of *Language and Communication* 25(1) (2005).

Collins, James, Stef Slembrouck and Mike Baynham (eds.). *Globalization and Languages in Context: Scale, Network, and Communicative Practice.* London: Continuum, 2011.

Conley, John M. and William M. O'Barr. 'The revictimization of rape victims.' *Just Words: Law, Language and Power.* Chicago: University of Chicago Press, 2005. 15–38.

Cooke, Michael. 'A different story: narrative versus "question and answer" in Aboriginal evidence.' *Forensic Linguistics* 3(2) (1996): 273–88.

Cotterill, Janet. 'Reading the rights: a cautionary tale of comprehension and comprehensibility.' *Forensic Linguistics* 7(1) (2000): 4–25.

Cotterill, Janet. ' "Just one more time ...": Change and continuity in courtroom narratives in the trials of OJ Simpson' *Language in the Legal Process.* Ed. Janet Cotterill. Basingstoke: Palgrave, 2002. 147–161

Cotterill, Janet. 'Collocation, connotation, and courtroom semantics: lawyers' control of witness testimony through lexical negotiation.' *Applied Linguistics* 25 (2004): 513–37.

Coulthard, Malcolm. 'On the use of corpora in the analysis of forensic texts.' *Forensic Linguistics* 1(1) (1994a): 27–43.

Coulthard, Malcolm. 'Powerful evidence for the defence: an exercise in forensic discourse analysis.' *Language and the Law.* Ed. John Gibbons. Harlow: Longman, 1994b. 414–27.

Coulthard, Malcolm. 'The official version: audience manipulation in police reports of interviews with suspects.' *Texts and Practices: Readings in Critical Discourse Analysis.* Eds. Carmen Caldas-Coulthard and R. Malcolm Coulthard. London: Routledge, 1996. 166–78.

Coulthard, Malcolm. 'A failed appeal.' *Forensic Linguistics* 4(2) (1997): 287–302.

Coulthard, Malcolm. 'Whose voice is it? Invented and concealed dialogue in written records of verbal evidence produced by the police.' *Language in the Legal Process.* Ed. Janet Cotterill. London: Palgrave, 2002. 19–34.

Coulthard, Malcolm. 'Author identification, idiolect and linguistic uniqueness.' *Applied Linguistics* 25(4) (2004): 431–47.

Coulthard, Malcolm. 'And then ... language description and author attribution.' 2006 http://www1.aston.ac.uk/lss/staff/coulthardm/ accessed 7 August 2013.

Crowley, Joe. 'A murderer, his medicine and a dose of statutory interpretation.' *The National Legal Eagle* 13(1) (2007): 7–10.

Crystal, David and Derek Davy. 'The language of legal documents.' *Investigating English Style.* Eds. David Crystal and Derek Davy. London: Longman, 1969. 193–217.

Danet, Brenda '"Baby" or "fetus"? Language and the construction of reality in a manslaughter trial.' *Semiotica* 32 (1980): 187–219.

Danet, Brenda and Bryna Bogoch. 'Orality, literacy, and performativity in Anglo-Saxon wills.' *Language and the Law.* Ed. John Gibbons. London: Pearson, 1994. 100–35.

Davis, Tom. 'ESDA and the analysis of contested contemporaneous notes of police interviews.' *Forensic Linguistics,* 1(1) (1994): 71–89.

de Saussure, Ferdinand. *Course in General Linguistics.* Eds. C. Bally and A. Sechehaye. Trans. A. Reidlinger and W. Baskin. London: McGraw Hill, 1966.

Deffenbacher, K.A., J.F. Cross, R.E. Handkins, J.E. Chance, A.G. Goldstein, R. Hammersley and J.D. Read. 'Relevance of voice identification research to criteria for evaluating reliability of an identification.' *The Journal of Psychology* 123 (1989): 109–19.

DeJongh, Elena M. *An Introduction to Court Interpreting: Theory and Practice.* Lanham, MD: University Press of America, 1992.

Di Paolo, Marianna and Georgia Green. 'Juror's beliefs about the interpretation of speaking style.' *American Speech, Special issue on Language, Variability and Law* 65(4) (1990): 304–22.

Diamond, Shari Seidman and Judith N. Levi. 'Improving decisions on death by revising and testing jury instructions.' *Judicature* 79(5) (1996): 224–31.

Doherty, Joe, Volker Busch-Geertsema, Vita Karpuskiene, Jukka Korhonen, Eoin O'Sullivan, Ingrid Sahlin, Antonio Tosi, Agostino Petrillo and Julia Wygna?ska. 'Homelessness and exclusion: regulating public space in European cities.' *Surveillance and Society* 5(3) (2008): 290–314.

Dumas, Bethany. 'US pattern jury instructions: problems and proposals.' *Forensic Linguistics* 7(1) (2000): 49–71.

Dumas, Bethany. 'Reasonable doubt about reasonable doubt: assessing jury instruction adequacy in a capital case.' *Language in the Legal Process.* Ed. Janet Cotterill. Basingstoke: Palgrave, 2002. 246–59.

Eades, Diana. 'Legal recognition of cultural differences in communication: the case of Robyn Kina.' *Language and Communication* 16(3) (1996): 215–27.

Eades, Diana. 'I don't think it's an answer to the question: silencing Aboriginal witnesses in court.' *Language in Society* 29(2) (2000): 161–95.

Eades, Diana. '"Evidence gained in unequivocal terms": gaining consent of aboriginal young people in court.' *Language in the Legal Process.* Ed. Janet Cotterill. Basingstoke: Palgrave, 2002. 162–79.

Eades, Diana. 'Participation of second language and second dialect speakers in the legal system.' *Annual Review of Applied Linguistics* 23 (2003): 113–33.

Eades, Diana. 'Applied linguistics and language analysis in asylum seeker cases.' *Applied Linguistics* 26(4) (2005): 503–26.

Eades, Diana. 'Language analysis and asylum cases.' *Handbook of Forensic Linguistics*. Eds. Malcolm Coulthard and Alison Johnson. Oxford: Routledge, 2010. 411–22.

Eagleson, Robert D. 'Forensic analysis of personal written texts: a case study.' *Language and the Law*. Ed. John Gibbons. Harlow: Longman, 1994. 362–73.

Elwork, Amiram, Bruce Dennis Sales and James J. Alfini. *Making Jury Instructions Understandable*. Charlottesville, VA: Michie, 1982.

English, Fiona. 'Non-native speakers in detention: assessing non-native speaking detainees' English language proficiency.' *Handbook of Forensic Linguistics*. Eds. Malcolm Coulthard and Alison Johnson. Oxford: Routledge, 2010. 432–9.

Ephratt, Michal. 'The functions of silence.' *Journal of Pragmatics* 40(11) (2008): 1909–38.

Evans, Betsy E. 'An acoustic and perceptual analysis of imitation.' *Handbook of Perceptual Dialectology II*. Eds. Daniel Long and Dennis R. Preston. Amsterdam: John Benjamins, 2002. 95–112.

Evans, Betsy E. 'Aspects of the analysis of imitation.' *Sociophonetics Handbook*. Eds. Dennis Preston and Nancy Niedzielski. Cambridge: Cambridge University Press, 2010. 379–92.

Faking News. 'Unable to attract even a single girl, frustrated man sues Axe.' 2009 http://www.fakingnews.firstpost.com/2009/10/unable-to-attract-even-a-single-girl-frustrated-man-sues-axe/ accessed 7 August 2013.

Filipovic, Luna. 'Language as a witness: insights from cognitive linguistics.' *International Journal of Speech, Language and the Law* 14(2) (2007): 245–67.

Foster, Peter. 'Exploding road sign: the true story.' *The Telegraph* 28 September 2009 http://blogs.telegraph.co.uk/news/peterfoster/100011571/exploding-road-sign-the-true-story/ accessed 7 August 2013.

Fox, Gwyneth. 'A comparison of "policespeak" and "normalspeak" a preliminary study.' *Techniques of Description: A Festschrift for Malcolm Coulthard*. Eds. John M. Sinclair, Michael Hoey and Gwyneth Fox. London: Routledge, 1993. 183–95.

Fraser, Bruce. 'Threatening revisited.' *Forensic Linguistics,* 5(2) (1998): 159–73.

Fraser, Helen. 'The role of "educated native speakers" in providing language analysis for the determination of the origin of asylum seekers.' *International Journal of Speech, Language and the Law* 16(1) (2009): 113–38.

French, Peter. 'An overview of forensic phonetics with particular reference to speaker identification.' *Forensic Linguistics* 1(2) (1994): 169–81.

French, Peter and Philip Harrison. 'Case report: R v Ingram, C., Ingram, D., and Whittock, T.' *International Journal of Speech, Language and the Law* 11(1) (2004): 131–45.

French, Peter and Philip Harrison. 'Position statement concerning use of impressionistic likelihood terms in speaker comparison cases with a foreword by Peter French and Philip Harrison.' *International Journal of Speech, Language and the Law* 14(1) (2007): 137–44.

French, Peter, Francis Nolan, Paul Foulkes, Philip Harrison and Kirsty McDougall. 'The UK position statement on forensic speaker comparison; a rejoinder to Rose and Morrison.' *International Journal of Speech, Language and the Law* 17(1) (2010): 143–52.

Gibbons, John. 'Revising the language of New South Wales police procedures: applied linguistics in action.' *Applied Linguistics* 22(4) (2001): 439–69.

Gibbons, John. *Forensic Linguistics: An Introduction to Language in the Justice System.* Oxford: Blackwell, 2003.

Goffman, Erving. *Forms of Talk.* Philadelphia: University of Pennsylvania Press, 1981.

Grant, Tim. 'Quantifying evidence in forensic authorship analysis.' *The International Journal of Speech, Language and the Law* 14(1) (2007): 1–25.

Grant, Tim. 'Text messaging forensics txt 4n6: idiolect free authorship analysis?' *Handbook of Forensic Linguistics.* Eds. Malcolm Coulthard and Alison Johnson. Oxford: Routledge, 2010. 508–22.

Grant, Tim. 'Txt 4n6: method, consistency, and distinctiveness in the analysis of SMS text messages.' *Journal of Law and Policy* 21(2), 467–94.

Gray, Peter R.A. 'The expert witness problem.' *International Journal of Speech, Language and the Law* 17(2) (2010): 201–9.

Green, David Allen. 'Twitter joke trial appeal – round-up of key links.'http://jackofkent.com/2012/06/twitterjoketrial-appeal-round-up-of-key-links/ accessed 7 August 2013.

Greenall, Annjo Klungervik. 'Towards a new theory of flouting.' *Journal of Pragmatics* 41 (2009): 2295–311.

Grice, H. Paul. 'Logic and conversation.' *Studies in the Way of Words.* London: Harvard University Press, 1989. 22–40.

Guardian. 'Corrections and clarifications.' 25 October 2004 http://www.guardian.co.uk/theguardian/2004/oct/25/correctionsandclarifications accessed 7 August 2013.

Gudjonsson, Gisli H. and John Pearse. 'Suspect interviews and false confessions.' *Current Directions in Psychological Science* 20(1) (2011): 33–7.

Gudjonsson, Gisli H. 'Unreliable confessions and miscarriages of justice in Britain.' *International Journal of Police Science and Management* 4(4) (2002): 332–43.

Hale, Sandra. 'Clash of world perspectives: the discursive practices of the law, the witness and the interpreter.' *Forensic Linguistics* 4(2) (1997): 197–209.

Hale, Sandra. 'How faithfully do court interpreters render the style of non-English speaking witnesses' testimonies? A data-based study of Spanish–English bilingual proceedings.' *Discourse Studies* 4(1) (2002): 25–47.

Hale, Sandra. 'The need to raise the bar. Court interpreters as specialized experts.' *Handbook of Forensic Linguistics*. Eds. Malcolm Coulthard and Alison Johnson. Oxford: Routledge, 2010. 440–54.

Halliday, Michael A.K. *An Introduction to Functional Grammar*. London: Edward Arnold, 1985.

Hankin, Susan. 'Statutory interpretation in the age of grammatical permissiveness: an object lesson for teaching why grammar matters.' 2010 http://digitalcommons.law.umaryland.edu/fac_pubs/892/ accessed 7 August 2013.

Harris, Sandra. 'Fragmented narratives and multiple tellers: witness and defendant accounts in trials.' *Discourse Studies* 3(1) (2001): 53–74.

Harris, Sandra. 'Telling stories and giving evidence: the hybridisation of narrative and non-narrative modes of discourse in a sexual assault trial.' *The Sociolinguistics of Narrative*. Eds Jennifer Coates and Joanna Thornborrow. Amsterdam: John Benjamins, 2004. 215–37.

Haworth, Kate. 'The dynamics of power and resistance in police interview discourse.' *Discourse and Society* 17(6) (2006): 739–59.

Heffer, Chris. ' "If you were standing in Marks and Spencers": narrativization and comprehension in the English summing-up.' *Language in the Legal Process*. Ed. Janet Cotterill. Basingstoke: Palgrave, 2002. 228–45.

Heffer, Chris. *The Language of Jury Trial: A Corpus-aided Analysis of Legal-Lay Discourse*. Basingstoke: Palgrave, 2005.

Heffer, Chris. 'Beyond "reasonable doubt": the criminal standard of proof instruction as communicative act.' *The International Journal of Speech, Language and the Law* 13(2) (2006): 159–88.

Heydon, Georgina. 'Establishing the structure of police evidentiary interviews with suspects.' *Forensic Linguistics* 11(1) (2004): 27–49.

Hill, James, Beth Lloyd and Russell Goldman. 'John Edwards feared wife's "volcanic" reaction to affair.' ABC News 14 May 2012 http://abcnews.go.com/Politics/john-edwards-feared-wifes-volcanic-reaction-affair/story?id=16341298 accessed 7 August 2013.

Hirson, Alan, J. Peter French and David Howard. 'Speech fundamental frequency over the telephone and face-to-face: some implications for forensic phonetics.' *Studies in General and English Phonetics: Essays in Honour of Professor J. D. O'Connor*. Ed. J. Windsor Lewis. London: Routledge, 1995. 230–40.

Hobbs, Pamela. 'Lawyers' use of humor as persuasion.' *Humor: International Journal of Humor Research* 20(2) (2007): 123–56.

Hoey, Michael. *Textual Interaction: An Introduction to Written Text Analysis*. London: Routledge, 2001.

Hot Coffee, Dir. Susan Saladoff. HBO, 2011. DVD.

Innes, Bronwen. 'R v. Bain – a unique case in New Zealand legal and linguistic history.' *International Journal of Speech Language and the Law*, 18(1) (2011): 145–55.

Jackson, Bernard. 'Narrative theories and legal discourse.' *Narrative in Culture: Storytelling in the Sciences, Philosophy and Literature.* Ed. Christopher Nash. London: Routledge, 1994. 23–50.

Jakobson, Roman. 'Closing statements: linguistics and poetics.' *Style in Language.* Ed. Thomas A. Sebeok. Cambridge, MA: MIT Press, 1960. 350–77.

Jaworski, Adam and Crispin Thurlow (eds.). *Semiotic Landscapes: Language, Image, Space.* London: Continuum, 2010.

Johnson, Michael G. 'Language and cognition in products liability.' *Language in the Judicial Process.* Eds. Judith N. Levi and Anne Graffam Walker. New York: Plenum, 1990. 291–308.

Judicial Studies Board. *Crown Court Bench Book: Directing the Jury,* 2010 http://www.judiciary.gov.uk/Resources/JCO/Documents/Training/benchbook_criminal_2010.pdf accessed 18 September 2012.

Karton, Joshua D.H. 'Lost in translation: international criminal courts and the legal implications of interpreted testimony.' *Vanderbilt Journal of Transnational Law* 41 (2008): 1–54.

Kerr Thompson, Joanna. ' "Powerful/powerless" language in court: a critical re-evaluation of the Duke Language and Law Programme.' *Forensic Linguistics* 9(2) (2002): 153–167.

Kimble, Joseph. 'Answering the critics of plain language.' *The Scribes Journal of Legal Writing* 5 (1994–5): 51–86, also at http://www.plainlanguage network.org/kimble/critics.htm accessed 7 August 2013.

Kleefeld, John C. 'From Brouhahas to Brehon laws: poetic impulse in the law.' *Law and Humanities* 4 (2010): 21–61.

Komter, Martha L. 'The suspect's own words: the treatment of written statements in Dutch courtrooms.' *Forensic Linguistics* 9(2) (2002): 168–92.

Komter, Martha L. 'The construction of records in Dutch police interrogations.' *Information Design Journal* 11(3) (2003): 201–13.

Komter, Martha L. 'From talk to text: the interactional construction of a police record.' *Research on Language and Social Interaction* 39(3) (2006): 201–28.

Kredens, Krzysztof and Ruth Morris. ' "A shattered mirror?" Interpreting in legal contexts outside the courtroom.' *Handbook of Forensic Linguistics.* Eds. Malcolm Coulthard and Alison Johnson. Oxford: Routledge, 2010. 455–69.

Kress, Gunther. *Multimodality: A Social Semiotic Approach to Contemporary Communication.* London: Routledge, 2010.

Kurzon, Dennis. ' "Legal Language": varieties, genres, registers, discourses.' *International Journal of Applied Linguistics,* 7(2) (1997): 119–39.

Kurzon, Dennis. 'Towards a typology of silence.' *Journal of Pragmatics* 39 (2007): 1673–88.

Labov, William. *Language in the Inner City.* Philadelphia: University of Pennsylvania Press, 1972.

Lacerda, Francisco. 'LVA-technology – the illusion of "lie detection." ' *Proceedings, FONETIK 2009, Dept. of Linguistics, Stockholm University* 2009 http://www2.ling.su.se/fon/fonetik_2009/220%20lacerda_fonetik2009.pdf accessed 7 August 2013..

LeGuin, Ursula.' Some thoughts on narrative.' *Dancing at the Edge of the World: Thoughts on Words, Women, Places.* London :Gollancz, 1992. 37–45.

Lakoff, George and Mark Johnson. *Metaphors We Live By.* Chicago: Chicago University Press, 1980.

Lakoff, Robin. *Language and Woman´s Place.* New York: Harper and Row, 1975.

Language and National Origin Group. 'Guidelines for the use of language analysis in relation to questions of national origin in refugee cases.' *International Journal of Speech Language and the Law* 11(2) (2004): 261–6.

Levi, Judith. 'Language as evidence: the linguist as expert witness in North American courts.' *Forensic Linguistics* 1(1) (1994): 1–26.

Levinson, Stephen C. 'Activity types and language.' *Talk at Work: Interaction in Institutional Settings.* Eds. Paul Drew and John Heritage. Cambridge: Cambridge University Press, 1992. 66–100.

Liberty. 'Liberty's response to the Home Office Consultation into procedures for voice identification techniques.' 2003. http://www.liberty-human-rights.org.uk/pdfs/policy03/nov-03-voice-identification-parade-response.pdf accessed 7 August 2013.

Linfoot-Ham, Kerry. 'Conversational maxims in encounters with law enforcement officers.' *International Journal of Speech, Language and the Law* 13(1) (2006): 23–54.

Locke, Jen. *Judicial Humour.* 2011 (updated 2013) https://lib.law.washington.edu/content/guides/judhumor accessed 7 August 2013.

Loftus, Elizabeth. 'Leading questions and the eyewitness report.' *Cognitive Psychology* 7 (1975): 550–72.

Loftus, Elizabeth. *Eyewitness Testimony,* 2nd edition. Cambridge, MA: Harvard University Press, 1996.

Luchjenbroers, June. 'In your own words …: questions and answers in a supreme court trial.' *Journal of Pragmatics* 27(4) (1997): 477–503.

Lucy, John. 'Linguistic Relativity.' *Annual Review of Anthropology* 26 (1997): 291–312.

Maley, Yon. 'The language of legislation.' *Language in Society* 16 (1987): 25–48.

Maret, Susan. *On Their Own Terms: A Lexicon with an Emphasis on Information-Related Terms Produced by the U.S. Federal Government.* 4th edition, revised November, 2010, http://www.fas.org/sgp/library/maret.pdf accessed 7 August 2013.

Marusek, Sarah. 'Wheelchair as semiotic: space governance of the American handicapped parking space.' *Law/Text/Culture* 9 (2005): 178–88.

Marusek, Sarah. 'Between disability and terror: handicapped parking space and homeland security at Fenway Park.' *International Journal for the Semiotics of Law* 20 (2007): 251–61.

Mautner, Gerlinde. 'Language, space and the law: a study of directive signs.' *International Journal of Speech Language and the Law* 19(2) (2012): 159–87.

McMenamin, Gerald R. 'Forensic stylistics: theory and practice of forensic stylistics.' *Handbook of Forensic Linguistics*. Eds. Malcolm Coulthard and Alison Johnson. Oxford: Routledge, 2010. 487–507.

McPeake, Robert (ed.). *Advocacy*, 15th edition. Oxford: Oxford University Press, 2010.

McShane, Larry. 'Judge sentences husband to buy wife flowers, take her out to dinner.' *New York Daily News* 8 February 2012 http://www.nydailynews.com/news/national/judge-sentences-husband-buy-wife-flowers-dinner-article-1.1019136 accessed 7 August 2013.

Meinhold, Stephen S. and David W. Neubauer. 'Exploring attitudes about the litigation explosion.' *The Justice System Journal* 22(2) (2001): 105–15.

Mellinkoff, David. *The Language of the Law*. Boston and Toronto: Little and Brown and Company, 1987.

Mooney, Annabelle. 'Co-operation, violations and making sense.' *Journal of Pragmatics* 36(5) (2004): 899–920.

Morris, Ruth. 'The gum syndrome: predicaments in court interpreting.' *Forensic Linguistics* 6(1) (1999): 6–29.

Namakula, Catherine S. 'Language Rights in the minimum guarantees of fair criminal trial.' *International Journal of Speech, Language and the Law* 19(1) (2012): 73–93.

Newbury, Phillip and Alison Johnson. 'Suspects' resistance to constraining and coercive questioning strategies in the police interview.' *International Journal of Speech, Language and the Law* 13(2) (2006): 213–40.

Nolan, Francis. 'Speaker identification evidence: its forms, limitations and roles.' *Proceedings of the Conference 'Law and Language: Prospect and Retrospect.'* Levi, Finnish Lapland, 2001. www.ling.cam.ac.uk/francis/LawLang.doc? accessed 7 August 2013.

Nolan, Francis. 'A recent voice parade.' *International Journal of Speech, Language and the Law* 10(2) (2003): 277–91.

O'Barr, William M. *Linguistic Evidence: Language, Power, and Strategy in the Courtroom*. New York: Academic Press, 1982.

O'Barr, William and Bowman Atkins. ' "Women's language" or "powerless language"?' *Women and Languages in Literature and Society*. Eds Sally McConnell-Ginet, Ruth Borker and Nelly Forman. New York: Praeger, 1980. 93–110.

O'Sullivan, Maureen. 'Unicorns or Tiger Woods: are lie detection experts myths or rarities? A response to on lie detection "Wizards" by Bond and Uysal', *Law and Human Behavior* 31(1) (2007): 117–23.

Obama, Barack. Oath of Office 2009 http://en.wikipedia.org/wiki/File:Barack_Obama_Oath_of_Office.ogg accessed 7 August 2013.

Olsson, John. 'The dictation and alteration of text.' *Forensic Linguistics* 4(2) (1997): 226–51.

Olsson, John. *Word Crime: Solving Crime through Forensic Linguistics.* London: Continuum, 2009.

Owen, Charles. 'Readability theory and the rights of detained persons.' *Recent Developments in Forensic Linguistics.* Ed. Hannes Kniffka, Frankfurt am Main: Peter Lang, 1996. 279–95.

Pavlenko, Aneta. ' "I'm very not about the law part": nonnative speakers of English and the Miranda warnings.' *TESOL Quarterly* 42(1) (2008): 1–30.

Peirce, Charles Saunders. *Semiotic and Significs: The Correspondence between Charles S. Peirce and Victoria Lady Welby.* Eds. Charles S. Hardwick and J. Cook. Bloomington: Indiana University Press, 1977.

Peirce, Charles Saunders. 'A syllabus of certain topics of logic.' *The Essential Peirce. Selected Philosophical Writings,* vol. 2 (1893–1913), Peirce Edition Project (ed.). Bloomington and Indianapolis: Indiana University Press, 1998.

Pomerantz, Anita. 'Agreeing and disagreeing with assessments: some features of preferred/dispreferred turn shapes.' *Structures of Social Action: Studies in Conversation Analysis.* Eds. J. Maxwell Atkinson and John Heritage. Cambridge: Cambridge University Press, 1984. 57–101.

Preston, Dennis. 'Linguistic profiling: the linguistic point of view'. *Language Allegiances and Bilingualism in the US.* Ed. M.R. Salaberry. Bristol: Multilingual Matters, 2009. 53–79.

Purnell, Thomas, William Idsardi and John Baugh. 'Perceptual and phonetic experiments on American English dialect identification.' *Journal of Language and Social Psychology* 18 (1999): 10–30.

Queensland Government. *The Queensland Legislation Handbook,* 4th edition. 2011 http://www.premiers.qld.gov.au/publications/categories/policies-and-codes/handbooks/legislation-handbook/assets/legislation-hand-book.pdf accessed 7 August 2013.

Reddy, Michael J. 'The conduit metaphor: a case of frame conflict in our language about language.' *Metaphor and Thought.* Ed. Andrew Ortony. Cambridge: Cambridge University Press, 1979. 284–310.

Rock, Frances. 'The genesis of a witness statement.' *Forensic Linguistics* 8(2) (2001): 44–72.

Rock, Frances. *Communicating Rights: The Language of Arrest and Detention.* Palgrave: Basingstoke, 2007.

Rose, Philip. 'Evaluation of disputed utterance evidence in the matter of David Bain's retrial.' Report prepared for court case, 23 February2009 http://rose-morrison.forensic-voice-comparison.net/publications.html accessed 13 August 2012.

Rose, Philip and Geoffrey Stewart Morrison. 'A response to the UK position statement on forensic speaker comparison.' *International Journal of Speech Language and the Law* 16(1) (2009): 139–63.

Sacks, Harvey, Emanuel A. Schegloff and Gail Jefferson. 'A simplest systematics for the organisation of turn-taking for conversation.' *Language*, 50 (1974): 696–735.

Scheffer, Thomas. 'On procedural discoursivation – or how local utterances are turned into binding facts.' *Language and Communication* 27 (2007): 1–27.

Schweitzer, N.J. and Michael J. Saks. 'The CSI effect: popular fiction about forensic science affects the public's expectations about real forensic science.' *Jurimetrics* 47 (2007): 357–64.

Scollon, Ron and Suzie Wong Scollon. *Discourses in Place: Language in the Material World.* London: Routledge, 2003.

Searle, John. 'Indirect speech acts.' *Syntax and Semantics, Vol. 3: Speech Acts.* Eds. Peter Cole and Jerry L. Morgan. New York: Academic Press, 1975. 59–82.

Shelton, Hon. Donald, Young S. Kim and Gregg Barak. 'A study of juror expectations and demands concerning scientific evidence: does the "CSI effect" exist?' *Vanderbilt Journal of Entertainment and Technology Law* 9(2) (2007): 331–68.

Shipman Archive 2005 http://webarchive.nationalarchives.gov.uk/2009 0808154959/http://www.the-shipman-inquiry.org.uk/home.asp accessed 7 August 2013.

Shohamy, Elana and Durk Gorter (eds.). *Linguistic Landscape: Expanding the Scenery.* London: Routledge, 2009.

Shon, Phillip Chong Ho. ' "I'd grab the S-O-B by his hair and yank him out the window": The fraternal order of warnings and threats in police–citizen encounters.' *Discourse and Society* 16(6) (2005): 829–45.

Shuy, Roger. 'Warning labels: language, law and comprehensibility.' *American Speech* 65(4) (1990): 291–303.

Shuy, Roger. *Language Crimes: The Use and Abuse of Language Evidence in the Courtroom.* Oxford: Blackwell, 1993.

Shuy, Roger. 'Ten unanswered language questions about Miranda.' *Forensic Linguistics* 4(2) (1997): 51–73.

Shuy, Roger. *Bureaucratic Language in Government and Business.* Washington DC: Georgetown University Press, 1998.

Shuy, Roger. 'DARE'S role in linguistic profiling.' *DARE Newsletter* 4(3) (2001): 1–5.

Siegel, Muffy E.A. 'Finding conversational facts: a role for linguistics in court.' *International Journal of Speech, Language and the Law* 12(2) (2005): 255–78.

The Simpson Trial Transcripts (TSTT), collected by Jack Walraven, http://walraven.org/simpson accessed 12 December 2012.

Simpson, Paul. *Language, Ideology and Point of View.* Oxford: Routledge, 1993.

Simpson, Paul. *Stylistics: A Resource Book for Students*. Oxford: Routledge, 2004.

Slapper, Gary and David Kelly. *The English Legal System*, 7th edition. Oxford: Routledge, 2004.

Slocum, Brian G. 'Linguistics and "ordinary meaning" determinations.' *Statute Law Review* 33(1) (2012): 39–83.

Sobkowiak, Wlodzimierz. 'Silence and markedness theory.' *Silence: Interdisciplinary Perspectives*. Ed. Adam Jaworski. Berlin: Mouton de Gruyter, 1997. 39–62.

Solan, Lawrence M. and Peter Tiersma. 'Author identification in the American Courts.' *Applied Linguistics* 25 (2004): 448–65.

Solomon, Nicky. 'Plain English: from a perspective of language in society.' *Literacy in Society*. Eds. Rugalya Hasan and Geoffrey Williams. London: Longman, 1996. 279–307.

Sperber, Dan and Deidre Wilson. *Relevance: Communication and Cognition*. Oxford: Blackwell, 1986.

Steyn, Mark. 'What's so funny about decapitation?' *The Telegraph* 26 October 2004 http://www.telegraph.co.uk/comment/personal-view/3612430/Whats-so-funny-about-decapitation.html accessed 7 August 2013.

Stokoe, Elizabeth and Derek Edwards. ' "Did you have permission to smash your neighbour's door?" Silly questions and their answers in police suspect interrogations.' *Discourse and Society* 10(1) (2008): 89–111.

Storey, Kate. 'The language of threats.' *Forensic Linguistics* 2(1) (1995): 74–80.

Stubbs, Michael. 'Judging the facts: an analysis of one text in its institutional context.' *Text and Corpus Analysis: Computer Assisted Studies of Language and Culture*. Ed. Michael Stubbs. Oxford: Blackwell, 1996. 101–24.

Sword, Helen. 'Zombie nouns.' *New York Times* Opinion 23 July 2012 http://opinionator.blogs.nytimes.com/2012/07/23/zombie-nouns/?smid=fb-share accessed 7 August 2013.

Thurlow, Crispin. 'Generation txt? The sociolinguistics of young people's text-messaging.' *Discourse Analysis Online* 1(1) (2003). http://extra.shu.ac.uk/daol/ accessed 12 December 2012.

Tiersma, Peter. *Legal Language*. Chicago: University of Chicago Press, 1999.

Tiersma, Peter. 'Textualizing the law.' *Forensic Linguistics* 8(2) (2001a): 73–92.

Tiersma, Peter. 'The rocky road to legal reform: improving the language of jury instructions.' *Brooklyn Law Review* 66(4) (2001b): 1081–119.

Tiersma, Peter. 'The language and law of product warnings.' *Language in the Legal Process*. Ed. Janet Cotterill. Palgrave: Basingstoke, 2002. 54–73.

Tiersma, Peter and Lawrence M. Solan. 'The linguist on the witness stand: linguistics in American courts.' *Language* 78(2) (2002): 221–39.

Toobin, Jeffrey. 'The CSI effect: the truth about forensic science.' *The New Yorker* 7 May 2007 http://www.newyorker.com/reporting/2007/05/07/070507fa_fact_toobin accessed 7 August 2013.

Transport for London, *Conditions of Carriage* http://www.tfl.gov.uk/assets/downloads/conditions-of-carriage-may-2012.pdf accessed 7 August 2013.

Trudgill, Peter. *Standard English,* 2011 http://www.phon.ucl.ac.uk/home/dick/SEtrudgill2011.pdf accessed 7 August 2013.

Tyrwhitt-Drake, Hugh. 'Massaging the evidence: the "overworking" of witness statements in civil cases.' *Forensic Linguistics* 10(2) (2003): 227–54.

United Nations. *Convention and Protocol Relating to the Status of Refugees,* 1951. http://www.unhcr.org/3b66c2aa10.html accessed 7 August 2013.

Valverde, Mariana. 'Taking "land use" seriously: toward an ontology of municipal law.' *Law/Text/Culture* 9 (2005): 34–59.

van der Vlis, Evert-Jan. 'The Right to Interpretation and Translation in criminal proceedings.' *The Journal of Specialised Translation* 14 (2010): 26–40.

van Leeuwen, Theo. 'Towards a semiotics of typography.' *Information Design Journal* 14(2) (2006): 139–55.

Wagner, Anne. 'The rules of the road: a universal visual semiotics.' *International Journal for the Semiotics of Law* 19(3) (2006): 311–24.

Wagner, Anne. 'French urban space management – a visual semiotic approach behind power and control.' *International Journal for the Semiotics of Law* 24(2) (2011): 227–42.

Watson-Brown, Anthony. 'In search of plain English – the Holy Grail or mythical Excalibur of legislative drafting.' *Statute Law Review* 33(1) (2012): 7–19.

Watt, Dominic. 'The identification of the individual through speech.' *Language and Identities.* Eds. Carmen Llamas and Dominic Watt. Edinburgh: Edinburgh University Press, 2010. http://www-users.york.ac.uk/~dw539/watt2009.pdf accessed 7 August 2013.

Whorf, Benjamin Lee. 'The relation of habitual thought and behaviour to language.' *Language, Meaning and Maturity: Selections from Etc., a Review of General Semantics,* 1943–1953. Ed. S.I. Hayakawa. New York: Harper, 1954. 197–215.

Wierzbicka, Anna. ' "Reasonable man" and "reasonable doubt": the English language, Anglo culture and Anglo-American law.' *International Journal of Speech Language and the Law* 10(1) (2003): 1–22.

Wodak, Ruth. 'The interaction between judge and defendant.' *Handbook of Discourse Analysis: Volume 4.* Ed. Teun van Dijk. London: Academic Press, 1985. 181–91.

Wolfram, Walt. 'Language ideology and dialect: understanding the Oakland ebonics controversy.' *Journal of English Linguistics* 26(2) (1998): 108–21.

Woodbury, Hanni. 'The strategic use of questions in court.' *Semiotica* 48(3/4) (1984): 197–228.

Yarmey, A. Daniel. 'Earwitness identification over the telephone and in field settings.' *International Journal of Speech Language and the Law* 10(1) (2003): 62–74.

Cases cited

Aveda Corp. v *Evita Marketing, Inc.*, 706 F. Supp. 1419 – Dist. Court, Minnesota 1989.

Chambers v *DPP* [2012] EWHC 2157 (Admin) http://www.bailii.org/ accessed 7 August 2013.

Clifford v *Commonwealth* (1999) Supreme Court of Kentucky. 97-SC-36 8-MR. Charles Clifford, Appellant, versus Commonwealth of Kentucky, Appellee. http://caselaw.findlaw.com/ky-supreme-court/1078989.html accessed 7 August 2013.

Liebeck v *McDonald's* No. CV 93 02419, 1995 WL 360309 (Bernalillo County, N.M. Dist. Ct. Aug. 18, 1994).

Miller v *Jackson* [1977] EWCA Civ 6 (06 April 1977).

R v *Derek William Bentley* (Deceased) [1998] EWCA Crim 2516 (30 July 1998) http://www.bailii.org/ accessed 7 August 2013.

Schenk v *Commissioner of Internal Revenue* 686 F2d 315 from http://openjurist.org/686/f2d/315/schenk-v-commissioner-of-internal-revenue accessed 7 August 2013.

Snyder v *Phelps et al.* 2011 U.S No. 09-751 http://www.supremecourt.gov/opinions/10pdf/09-751.pdf accessed 7 August 2013.

Legislation

Bribery Act (UK) 2010

Criminal Justice and Police Act (UK) 2001

Criminal Justice and Public Order Act (UK) 1994

Licensing Act (UK) 2003

Offences Against the Person Act (UK) 1861

Theft Act (UK) 1968

Trustee Act (UK) 2000

Websites

All accessed 7 August 2013

Australasian Legal Information Institute, www.austlii.edu.au/

British and Irish Legal Information Institute, www.bailii.org/

Fuzzy Law, http://fuzzylaw.cardiff.ac.uk/terms

The Law Dictionary, http://thelawdictionary.org

Legal Information Institute, www.law.cornell.edu

Index